Ackno

Praise God from whom all blessings flow....

Many thanks to those that have encouraged me to keep writing throughout the years. And many thanks to the many people that have walked with me throughout the difficult journey of life. I could not have done this without your help, continued encouragement, and many blessings. May God bless each of you ten-fold for the blessing you are to me!

All Scripture quoted within this book is from the New King James Version, unless otherwise noted.

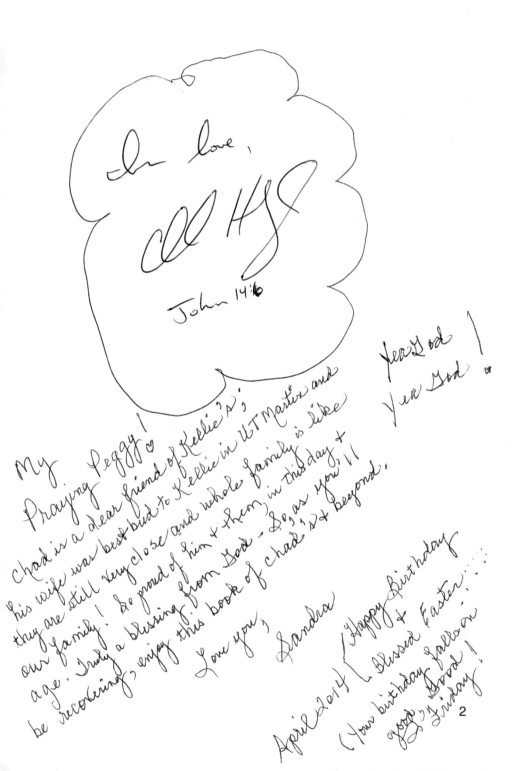

In love,
Chad HJ

John 14:6

My Praying Peggy!

Chad is a dear friend of Kellie's;
his wife was best bud to Kellie in UT Martin and
they are still very close and whole family is like
our family! So proud of him & them, in this day &
age. Truly a blessing from God - So as you'll
be recieving? enjoy this book of Chad's & beyond.

Yea God!
Yea God!

Love you,
Sandra

April 2014 (Happy Birthday
& Blessed Easter...
(Your birthday falls on
Good Friday

Introduction

And seeing the multitudes, He went up on a mountain, and when He was seated His disciples came to Him. Matthew 5:1

The *Sermon on the Mount* is found in chapters 5-7 in the book of *Matthew*. It is the first exposed teaching of Jesus to His new disciples. What we find in the chapters prior to this teaching is the account of Jesus' life before ministry, His baptism by John the Baptist, His empowerment of the Holy Spirit, His forty days of fasting and temptation, the calling of His disciples and the gathering of the multitudes. Once the multitudes had gathered unto Jesus, due to the miracle workings of His hands, He pulls the disciples aside and instructs them. You and I will do well to understand the significance of this. This teaching is directed to the follower of Christ, not the multitudes. But as you will see, the multitudes will turn an ear to these teachings for they are the truth that man's heart ultimately longs for.

When God placed it on my heart to do this devotional series, I had no idea of the length of time it would take me to walk through three chapters in Matthew. I simply started a journey with Him and asked Him for understanding. When I finished the task set before me, I was amazed that it ended up taking forty days. Looking back at the time of this writing, I encountered some significant struggles throughout the forty days it took me to write it. You may also encounter some natural struggles. But I encourage you to press through! For the experience and understanding gained through these forty days has far surpassed the difficulty encountered during the testing.

There is a spiritual significance to the number forty within the Bible. Let's look at just a few examples of this number being used by God. When the rain fell in the days of Noah, which flooded the earth, it rained for forty days and nights (*Genesis 7:4*). Moses spent forty years in the wilderness before being called by God to lead the Israelites into the Promised Land (*Acts 7:30*). The Israelites spent 40 years in the desert before entering the Promised Land (*Numbers 14*). Moses spent forty days and nights on two different occasions in God's Presence in order to receive the Ten Commandments (*Exodus 24 & 34*). Goliath presented himself before Israel for forty days before David slew him (*1 Samuel 17:16*). Through Jonah, God offered forty days to Nineveh for a time of repentance (*Jonah 3:4*). Jesus spent forty days and nights in the wilderness fasting and being tempted (*Matthew 4:2 & Luke 4:2*).

So, what do we gain from these examples? The number forty is a number of testing and trial. It is God's determined time as a proving ground of faith. I encourage you to not overlook the significance of this truth. Without preconceived idea or determination, I asked God to walk me through the Sermon on the Mount. And through the days that it took to write it, I was constantly broken before God. I was tempted to flee from my endeavor, but I was also greatly encouraged to press on. And when I finished, forty days had passed. I pray that the forty days it takes you to press through these words are significant to you. I encourage you to not take more than one day at a time. For I am confident that my spiritual walk has been greatly increased through the process that I have endured.

So, why the Sermon on the Mount? As I began reading books from Bible teachers from past centuries, I came across an important truth that they each shared. They saw a special significance within this initial teaching of Jesus. Chuck Smith, the founder of Calvary Chapel churches, refers to this teaching as the Great Manifesto of the Christian faith. Dietrich Bonhoeffer stated that this one passage should have the greatest significance on a Christian's life. Over the ages, spiritual giants have many times gone back to this teaching and stated the incredible impact that it has had on their lives. With that in mind, let's dive in....

Up to this point, the disciples had left everything and followed Jesus. They immediately saw the power of Jesus, but for the first time on record, He was about to really flip their world upside down. Isn't it funny how true faith in Christ does that to every one of us? As we grow in faith, all that we had previously valued no longer holds the same significance. Social position, personal wealth, independence and keeping all the rules will not guarantee us peace or satisfaction. What's more, they will not lead us to salvation. Jesus doesn't say that you have to do all these things in order to be a true follower. He simply lays them out before His disciples as a guide. The only thing that can bring us salvation is faith in Jesus. But how we live after that makes the difference on what impact we have on the world around us and how we mature in our relationship with the Master.

Look back to the verses that started this introduction. We see that Jesus saw the multitudes and went up the mountain. This is significant. Most people won't follow Jesus when the walk becomes difficult. They want the blessings of Jesus, but they aren't willing to endure what it takes to become intimate with Him. Therefore, they stay on the wide road. They stay in the valleys. Whenever our path in this world becomes arduous or difficult, we should see it as a distinct calling of God into a greater intimacy with Him. We must be willing to walk where others won't. That gets us alone with God. And within the alone times, we find the greatest intimacy.

Also notice that there was a distance between Jesus and the disciples. It wasn't until He was seated that they came to Him. Most Christians seem to live their life with a distance between themselves and Jesus. But we are called to intimacy. I can see myself as a spectator in this situation between Jesus and His disciples. Jesus sees the mass of people starting to press in, and so He starts walking an unfamiliar path. The disciples curiously follow Him, questioning one another as to where He is going. As He continues to climb, some were probably questioning the point of this journey. Others were probably still relishing the miracles of the days before. Either way, none could have expected what true intimacy with Christ involves. As we enter into this teaching over the next bit of time, let us not presuppose that which we will receive. Rather, let us come open-minded, just seeking instruction from our Father as taught by Jesus. Buckle up friends, we're about to take a heck of a ride!

Today's Prayer

Father, thank You for calling me into intimacy with You. Thank You for opening my eyes and calling me to Yourself. Thank You for giving me purpose and for Your willingness to pour Yourself within me. I do not take this calling nonchalantly. I see that You desire to bring me closer to You and to use me to be a light to others. As I see the needs around me, I see that You are looking at the spiritual bankruptcy of all people. We need restructuring. We need to be realigned to Your principles and truth. We need salvation. Father, help me to not be satisfied only with salvation, but only with a lasting and continually vibrant relationship with You. Thank You for turning my world upside down. Help me and encourage me as I adjust to this different way of living. In Jesus' name, Amen!

Day One

Opening the Kingdom of Heaven

<u>Today's Word</u>
Then He opened His mouth and taught them, saying: "Blessed are the poor in spirit, for theirs is the kingdom of heaven." *Matthew 5:2-3*

<u>Today's Thought</u>
With the understanding of yesterday's introduction, let's get into the meat of this calling of all Christians. The first thing I notice here is that when the disciples came to Jesus, He opened His mouth and taught them. When we approach Jesus, He never remains silent. We may not be in a place to hear Him, but He surely speaks. He speaks not to our ears; but rather, He chooses to speak to our hearts. And the words with which He speaks offer us life. They may shake us to our core, but it is because we are a new creation and must be retrained as to the principles which really matter. More than anything else you gain from this word today, know that Jesus wants to talk with you. All we have to do is approach Him with an open heart.

Next, we enter into the Beatitudes. In these simple, proverbial teachings, Jesus turns our world upside down. No longer are we to live by all the standards that man has ingrained within our spirits. We are to live for something more. And by living in the manner which we are about to explore, Jesus assures us that blessings will surround us. Better yet, we shall live in blessing and be a blessing to others. So, let's dive in to the first one.

Blessed are the poor in spirit, for theirs is the kingdom of heaven.

Remember when Jesus told the disciples that unless they became like the little children, they could not enter into the Kingdom of Heaven? That was an echo of this teaching. I am sure it resonated with the disciples, but does it resonate with you and I? Being poor in spirit does not mean financially poor. Taking a vow of poverty in order to seem more spiritually fit is a self-righteous doctrine. For God gives financial wealth to men according to His purpose. Being poor in spirit is something entirely different. It means having a proper understanding of our own inadequacy. We must have a right perspective. We have no power to obtain God. But through submission, we are gifted Him. Through the work of the cross, we are offered salvation.

Look into the life of Jesus and you will see that He was fully dependent on God. Over and over again, Jesus shared this. When asked by what authority He did the things He did, He replied, "*I*

only do that which I see my Father doing."
Children are dependent on others for their very
sustenance. So also, should we be dependent on
God for our very being. When we get this, God
offers the entirety of Heaven to us. You see, we
must empty ourselves before God so that He can
fill us with the kingdom of Heaven.

Lastly, we must know that the kingdom of heaven
is for us in the here and now. The glory of
Heaven surely awaits all believers when this
earthly journey is done, but God wants to deposit
the very same kingdom, or power, within us here
and now. How are we to be the light of the world
unless we are filled with the everlasting light of
Christ? This is the glory of Heaven, the land
where there are no shadows. We are always
enlightened. We are not to walk through this
world in darkness, but in the light of Christ. So,
may we begin to comprehend the vastness of
nothingness. May we all become poor in spirit.

Today's Prayer
Father, thank You for always speaking to me.
Thank You for not remaining silent in
condemnation or judgment. You seek to bless me
and enlighten me, and I realize that. You desire
for me to open my heart entirely to You so that
You can indwell within me. You want to fill me to
the point of overflowing! Lord, I am dependent on
You. You are the air I breathe. You are my life.

Lord, speak to this heart of mine and cause me to understand the principles of Kingdom living. I empty myself before You and accept the sacrifice of the cross. Pour out Your Spirit unto me, just as Your Word promises and cause this new creation to flourish! I bless You because of how much You bless me! Thank You Jesus! Thank You Holy Spirit! And thank You Father God! It is through Your Son Jesus that I am able to commune with You like this and in His name that I offer this incense before You, Amen!

Day Two

The Beautiful Pain

Today's Word
Blessed are those who mourn, for they shall be comforted. *Matthew 5:4*

Today's Thought
Again we see that the Kingdom of God seems upside down from the kingdom of earth. Here on earth, we do all that we can to avoid any sadness or stress. We strive to make our lives easier. We close our eyes to the things that are hard to look at and turn away from the things which cause us grief. But Jesus says that we are blessed when we mourn. The greek word for mourn means a deep, intensive sorrow, or a lamentation.

Here sits Jesus, in the same area that Jeremiah was when he wrote the book of Lamentations. Jeremiah wrote that book while weeping over the destruction of Jerusalem. Lamentations was very important to the Jews, and I am confident that this reference perked the ears of Jesus' disciples. You see, each year in synagogues across the world, Lamentations is read and the falling of Jerusalem is remembered. And since that desperate time, Jews had prayed for a redeemer to come and re-establish Jerusalem as the righteous city of God. They had been eagerly awaiting their Savior and King, and here He sat in front of them.

I have often judged the disciples as ignorant and foolish for not recognizing all that Jesus was trying to do in and through them. I have often identified my own struggles in theirs as well. I imagine that as children, the disciples had grown up hearing stories over the dinner table of the coming of a King that would make everything better. And so far in their journey, they had definitely seen many good works of Jesus. They must have been thinking that the continuous prayers of the Jews over the centuries had finally been answered. I think this is the first time that their hearts began being turned to thinking that Jesus was here to establish His authority. And they were going to be His Chief Counsel! Oh, how right they were; but their hearts would need to be kneaded over the next three to four years so that they could step into the office for which Jesus was preparing them.

How often have I asked for Jesus to step into a situation so that He could make everything better? But this is not what Jesus promises here. He says that we are blessed when we mourn. Through mourning, we shall find comfort. The greek word for comfort here means to be summoned to one's side. Godly sorrow produces repentance, or change in one's heart. Essentially,

Jesus is saying that when we are deeply sorrowful, we are called to the side of the Father. Sorrow brings us intimately closer to God. Now, let's look into the type of things that should produce this intense sorrow.

Just like Jeremiah, we know that Jesus was sorrowful when He looked over Jerusalem. He saw the spiritual condition God's children and the destruction that followed. Our hearts should literally break when we look at the situation of the Western world. The lands which once stood as a beacon of hope and light have now become spiritually dull. The spiritual lights that gleam are spread out and far in-between. There is a need for national repentance within North America and Europe. But what I see, even within the Christian communities, is worry over our retirement accounts, the environment, our way of life. These things are important, but they should hold no significance in comparison to the decay of our spiritual condition.

Whether it be the loss of a loved one, the pride and self-righteous spirit that seems so prevalent in today's world, or the spiritual deadness of our own hearts or those around us, we should be able to mourn. We are called to be a joyful people, full of light and hope, but somewhere within our quiet time, our hearts should break at the spiritual condition of our world. And that sorrow, if we're willing to accept it, will bring us closer to the heart of God. And we shall be blessed for it.

Today's Prayer

Father, oh how dull my senses often are! Forgive me for being so content in my own situation and not seeing the world around me as You see it. I know that You look at the sinful state of mankind in today's world and Your heart aches. You are not angry in judgment, but I know You to simply want blessing to reign about our lands. You want to heal, yet our hearts remain so far from You. Forgive me for not perceiving this. Forgive me for turning a blind eye at the desperate situation of the world around me. Lord, I cling to You in sorrow. I search You out in desperation. Heal me of my indifference! Continue to heal my heart so that I might reflect You accurately. In Jesus name, Amen!

Day Three

Our Inheritance

Today's Word
Blessed are the meek, for they shall inherit the earth. *Matthew 5:5*

Today's Thought
Meekness is one of those things that many people like to describe, but so few actually have a firm enough grasp on it that they may live it. Chuck Smith says that it is best to perhaps put a hyphen in the middle of the word me-ek. In other words, part of the principle of being meek is to take our eyes off of ourselves because we understand that any of our own efforts will get us nowhere. But perhaps the best understanding of meekness is stated by Peter Kreeft in *Back to Virtue*. He says, "*To see what meekness is, you must look not at meekness but at Christ. Saying meekness is this or that sends you to concepts which are pale copies of reality. Saying 'Jesus is meek' sends you to the living reality of it.*"

So far in our study of the Beatitudes, we have learned of the importance of being poor in spirit, having a broken heart towards this broken world, and now we see the importance of understanding just how blessed we can be when we have a proper perspective of ourselves in relation to God.

But in order to gain full understanding of meekness, we must look at the entirety of this verse. It is the meek that shall inherit the earth. We know that God is not in the business of giving us broken things, He's in the business of healing broken things. So what earth is Jesus talking about here?

The earth that the meek shall inherit is the new earth that Jesus talks about in Revelation. It is the restored earth that shall be as it was intended to be. It will be glorious and beyond our wildest imagination. Another key word to understand here is inherit. The meek shall be given the gloriousness of God. You see, there's nothing that we can do to earn God's gifts. We cannot take it by force, for we are weak in comparison. The key to obtaining anything Godly is to empty ourselves of everything worldly. For only when we are poured out like the drink offering that Jesus is, can we begin to receive. We cannot obtain, only receive.

To take it back to what Peter Kreeft said, our only hope for meekness and therefore the inheritance of God's gloriousness, is to be more like Jesus. Our eyes must be taken off of ourselves and placed onto the people that God has placed around us. Jesus looked to the Father for guidance in everything. He was empowered by the Holy Spirit for everything. And He willingly gave His everything for others, even those that did not appreciate nor were willing to receive. How different would our world look if all those that professed with their lips faith in Jesus Christ actually embodied the Spirit and mindset of our Savior?

Meekness is a much bigger concept than one day's devotional. And I know that I ,for one, will spend the rest of my life trying to deepen my understanding of this one characteristic of Godliness. Nevertheless, we cannot grow disheartened nor view this as something unobtainable. It is only unobtainable if we seek to grasp it by our own efforts. In my relationship with Jesus, I am beginning to truly understand that I can only grasp by first letting go. May we all have the submissive spirit within ourselves to follow our Master's example. Not for a deeper sense of holiness or some sort of spiritual pride, but because intimacy and depth call us to it.

Today's Prayer
Father, I am so thankful that You continually draw me in closer to You. But even in saying that, I realize how far I am away from You! Lord, I need You more. And I need You now! Help me let go of all that hinders me from fullness in You. As You turn my world upside down, help me to allow Your full process of transformation take hold and make me like Your Son Jesus. I know that all of this is

fully available, if I will only let go. Help me understand the detriment of those things that I allow to take priority in my life over You. I am weak, but in You, I am strong. Therefore, I will not grow weary, nor will I lose heart. In Christ alone, I will place my trust. I will echo the words of the young virgin Mary who bore Your earthly Son when I say, "Let it be with me just as You have said." In Jesus' name and by His blood I pray, Amen!

Day Four

Blessed are the Hungry

Today's Word
Blessed are those who hunger and thirst for righteousness, for they shall be filled.   *Matthew 5:6*

Today's Thought
Oh, what a blessing to come to this scripture today! The first three beatitudes leave me feeling inadequate, for I have the wherewithal to understand that my own self-righteousness is at best corrupt and manipulated.   I long for something so much greater!   Here I am, only three sentences into Jesus' great teaching, and I am longing for a Savior!   I am neither poor in spirit, mournful, nor meek and I realize that I need these qualities in my life. But how do I get there? And so carries on our Master with His great teaching....

Blessed are those who hunger and thirst for righteousness.   I cannot obtain the treasures of Christ by my own efforts, for they are a gift held firm within His grasp and only doled out as the Holy Spirit decides. Faced with the inadequacies of my own abilities, I am hungry and thirsty for more than merely living. I am craving life itself. Now, Jesus brings hope to our hearts.   *Psalm*

19:7 says *"The law of the LORD is perfect, converting the soul. The testimony of the LORD is sure, making wise the simple..."* As sure as Jesus is the Living Word, so also does He pierce my heart with such perfect statements that expose my own failure. And my realization of this failure creates thirst within me. I had no idea what a sinner I was until I was faced with the perfection of God. In His light, I am awakened.

We all hunger and thirst. But is it righteousness that we long so desperately for? If I choose to live apart from God, I will only hunger and thirst for those things which bring me temporal relief from my longing. I will continually lust for things that I do not have. But here, Jesus offers us peace from such longing. Jesus assures us that if we hunger for the right things, we shall be filled. And that process of His filling brings satisfaction to our souls. It alleviates the pain of longing, for we realize that we are complete only in Christ. And that creates a greater longing to know Him more! And the beautiful thing about that is that we know that we can never exhaust the riches and gloriousness of Christ (*Romans 11:33*)!

Here's the kicker. I have known many men and women that have rested on their past pursuits of Jesus. And because their past pursuits produced great fruit, they felt as though they had arrived at some level of spiritual enlightenment. But the second that we stop searching for greater treasures, we start becoming self-righteous. We stop depending on the satisfaction of God and start gaining knowledge that deceives us into thinking that we are still on the right track.

The path of the true Christian is one of continual discovery and brokenness. We must be willing to allow God full access into every part of our being so that we can be filled. During a worship service, I once had this vision of a dimly lit interior of a castle. As I walked the hallways of my own castle, I came across a locked door. I made my way into the room beyond the door, quickly locking the door behind me. In this room were great treasures. Some of my most prized possessions lay hidden within this protected vault. Then God spoke to my heart and let me know that there were treasures within my heart to which I would not grant Him access. Although they may not have been impure within themselves, I, and they, would become corrupted if I did not grant Him full access within my heart. There can be no locked doors. For if I keep things locked behind closed doors, it was because I do not trust Him with them. And that lack of trust would corrupt me and poison the things that I so greatly treasured.

Longing and thirsting for righteousness should be a life-long pursuit. If we get to the point where this verse of Jesus does not pierce us, then we must expose ourselves to more of His Word. For the Word is the Light that exposes our own inadequacies and mistrust. This process is painful, for we must learn to offer up our most prized possessions. And in that sacrifice of our offering, we shall be greatly blessed.

Today's Prayer

Father, oh how You pierce my heart and expose my desperate need for You! I am so thankful that You open my eyes to Your truth! Lord, I need You more today than yesterday. I welcome Your forgiveness and Your love which casts away all fear and worry. I invite You fully into my heart. The castle of my soul is opened to You. Fill me with Your Great Holy Spirit! I feel Your Presence and it brings me peace. I have tasted and know that You are indeed good. For there is no evil within You. Mold me according to Your Will. Refine me in Your fire of pure love. In Jesus' name, Amen!

Day Five

Jesus on Mercy

<u>**Today's Word**</u>
Blessed are the merciful, for they shall obtain mercy. *Matthew 5:7*

<u>**Today's Thought**</u>
Blessed are the merciful, for they shall obtain mercy. Oh, how quickly we could pass over the significance of this statement by our Master! Mercy has become one of those Christian bywords that we read over quickly as though we have already grasped the importance of this characteristic within the true believer's life. What is mercy? And how do we obtain it?

I want to share with you something that I came across on *blueletterbible.org*, which is a phenomenal free Bible study website. The following paragraph is from Chuck Smith's study on the Sermon on the Mount. It is too good to try to summarize it or not share in it's entirety.

"Justice is getting what we deserve. Mercy is not getting what we deserve. Grace is getting what we don't deserve. After being filled, we become the next three Beatitudes. Because we have received the mercy of God through repentance, we can be merciful. If we aren't merciful, we haven't actually received God's mercy. Those who have received forgiveness show forgiveness. The Greek word for "mercy" has its root in the Hebrew word meaning "to get inside someone else's skin." This means that you can totally identify with what he's seeing, thinking, and feeling (*Ezekiel 3:15*). God came into the skin of man through Christ to be able to identify with us. Sympathy is to suffer together or to experience together the pains and sufferings of others (*Luke 10:30-37*). The Gospel places the emphasis on what we are, not on what we are doing (*Ephesians 1-4*). Because of this, the call to action is wrong. If we're what God wants us to be, we'll do what God wants us to do (*Galatians 2:20; 2 Corinthians 5:17*)." -Chuck Smith

Do you see where the importance lies? Whatsoever we have personally experienced will begin to take root in our lives, and we will reproduce the very same fruit of which we have already eaten. This is a universal truth. Paul tells us in *Galatians 6:7*, "*Do not be deceived, God is not mocked; for whatever a man sows, that he will also reap.*" Others have called this karma, and here we see it in Biblical truth.

Jesus blesses those that are merciful; for they have a true realization of the mercy of God in their own lives. Jesus repeated this principle when He said that those without sin should cast the first stone. You see, if we have been forgiven much, we will forgive others. We will be more compassionate towards others because we understand how wretched we are in our own condition apart from God. It is by His mercy that I awake in newness of life each and every day. Therefore, I will live my life with as little judgment as I can possibly proclaim on others. And it is my desire to never judge others because I understand the Biblical principle that with whatever measure I judge others, God Himself will judge me.

When will I truly learn that these important principles which Jesus is sharing is about changing my own heart? Oh, the impact that the Gospel could have on the world around us if we simply allowed it to complete its' work in our own lives! That's how Jesus changed the world. He lived within the will of the Father. He embodied the Father's compassion toward us and demonstrated the Father's love for us by laying down His own life for our sins. A compassionate Christian is one that understands the Gospel. Truly, if one has experienced the mercy of God, he has no choice but to be merciful towards others. And to this end, shall I live openly by the grace of God.

Today's Prayer
Father, oh, how merciful You are towards me! You choose to remember my sins no more! You have opened my eyes to Your truth and You call me to live openly before others. You choose to

operate within me despite my own failings and judgmental views of others. Lord, forgive me! Have mercy on me! Father, empower me, just as You empowered Jesus with the Holy Spirit, so that I may continue this journey into the depths of my own heart. I long to be more like You. I long to experience Your fullness in my life. And I know that I have so often twisted and manipulated Your Word for my own benefit and self-righteousness. I am nothing without You. I need You more every hour! Thank You for working on this sinful man and for transferring the righteousness of Your Son Jesus upon me. I don't deserve it. But I so happily welcome it! Lord, You amaze me with Your love. You truly speak to me in ways that man cannot perceive. Lord, may Your will be made perfect in my life, for to You alone do I lay down my life. Continue to convict me for Your instruction is sweet and full of mercy! In Jesus' wonderful name I pray, Amen!

Day Six

I Want to See God

Today's Word

Blessed are the pure in heart, for they shall see God. *Matthew 5:8*

Today's Thought

What a wonderful promise our Master offers us this morning! Those that are pure in heart shall see God. As I read and contemplate this promise today, my mind becomes curious as to the wording which Jesus uses. Why is it that those that are pure in heart shall see God? Should it not be those that are pure in vision? Should we not be honing our very senses that the Lord has provided us with so that we may experience God more?

I know of no one that is on their spiritual path with Jesus that would not want to see Him more clearly. Regularly, I hear others say that they want to know God's will for their lives. And the way to know God's will is to know Him. What seems surprising, because of the nature of independent man which is ingrained within us, is that there is nothing we can do through our own efforts to get closer to God. Our pursuit of God can only get us to our destination when we give up. When we realize that our best efforts to obtain God are foolish and lead us nowhere but deeper into self-righteousness, then we are beginning to understand.

This is why Jesus says that it is the pure of heart that shall see God. We must be cleansed by God Himself in order to become pure. And that takes submission to His Lordship and all of His glorious processes. Paul speaks to this in his letter to the Church at Ephesus when he addresses how husbands ought to love their wives. In chapter 5, verses 25-27, he writes: *"Husbands, love your wives, just as Christ also loved the church and gave Himself for her, that He might sanctify and cleanse her with the washing of water by the word, that He might present her to Himself a glorious church, not having spot or wrinkle or any such thing, but that she should be holy and without blemish."* Just as it is the responsibility of the husband to look over his wife, so also is it Jesus' responsibility to look over us. But if a wife refuses to submit to her husband, then no work can be done by the husband. If we, as followers of Jesus, refuse to submit to Him, then He cannot complete His work of love within us. So this process is an effort of complemented submission. How beautiful is that picture?

The real question we must each ask ourselves is "Do I love and trust Jesus?" The wife that trusts her husband submits to him willingly, for she sees first and foremost that he has already submitted himself to her. Likewise, the Christian that has truly experienced the love and light of Christ in his or her own life knows that there is not a more secure and trustworthy place than within the embrace of our Lord. Therefore, we submit in full trust.

Using the same verses in Ephesians, we can see that the process of purification which leads to purity of our hearts is through the washing of water by the word. The Greek translation for "word" here is *rhema*. And in this context, it means the enjoining of two. When someone washes another, it is an intimate process. I think of when my wife has asked me to wash her back while she's in the bathtub. It has very little to do with getting any dirt off of her skin. And it has everything to do with me accepting her as she is. It is a call to be loved. We all want to be loved. And we must be willing to submit to Christ in our own nakedness, asking Him to wash us as He sees fit. It is not cleansing that we are truly seeking, it is simply His love, His absolute acceptance. And Jesus promises us that if we are willing to intimately ask Him into our lives like that, He will accept us. We have nothing to fear.

The pure in heart shall see God. Those that are fully submitted to God, in full trust and without precondition, shall know Him more intimately.

And oh, what a glorious blessing awaits us! I love how Paul completed this thought in *Ephesians 5:27*! Through this process of love and complemented submission, we shall be presented before Jesus without spot, blemish or wrinkle! The language here truly hits home. I look at the amount of money that people spend in order to rid themselves of wrinkles and supposed imperfections that they identify on their bodies. All of those efforts are futile, because they will not bring us that for which we truly desire. Deep down, we all want to be loved, warts and all. And that is the very love that Jesus is promising us here through this Beatitude. And that, my friends, is living the blessed life!

Today's Prayer
Father, oh, how I trust You more and more! I truly see the unconditional love that You offer me. I accept the salvation that Jesus offers me. I drop my reservations that have kept You at a distance because I have been afraid that You would not accept me fully if I revealed all of my yuck to You. Lord, You love me without hesitance. You accept me fully! Lord, how sweet and wonderfully true You are! Wash me and present me pure before Yourself. For within this process, I am beginning to truly taste Your incomparable love for me. Have Your way! In Jesus' name, Amen!

Day Seven

Being His Child

Today's Word

Blessed are the peacemakers, for they shall be called sons of God. *Matthew 5:9*

Today's Thought

Those who bring peace shall be called sons of God. What an offering the Master holds before us. As with all Jesus' teachings, there are a multiplicity of levels on which we can understand this. First, we must remember that all of these Beatitudes shared by Jesus and offered unto us were first truly embodied in Himself. Jesus was the demonstration. And He was fully human. He offers us a better way of living, which is fully obtainable through our submission to Him. It will cause us to die to ourselves, but that is part of the blessing!

The first thing I thought of when I read this verse this morning is that just before this, Jesus was identified as the Son of God. Do you remember what we first discussed in the introduction to the Sermon on the Mount? This is Jesus' first recorded teaching. He had been baptized by John the Baptist. The Holy Spirit descended upon Him as a dove. And a voice came from heaven and stated, "*This is My Beloved Son, in whom I am well pleased.*" Jesus had already been identified publicly as God's Son.   If the disciples were anything like me, they too longed for such a declaration.   So their ears had to be perked at this statement of Jesus.   I can see myself sitting amongst the twelve, my heart would've leaped within my chest and my head would've shouted within me- "I want to be a son of God!"

The second thing I think about is how it is recorded in *Mark 3*, that James and John were called the sons of thunder. Jesus gave them this nickname Himself.   I wonder what their hearts must have felt when they heard this statement. For if Jesus had already given them this nickname, surely they must have felt some conviction at this point. Think of it this way. No one truly knows why Jesus gave them this nickname, but many speculate that it was because of their fiery and bold preaching style. James was the first disciple to be martyred for Christ and John was the last disciple to remain alive. In this, these two brothers bookended the start of the Christian Church. And while their zeal and boldness is to be commended, Jesus was after their hearts.

To me, what I am being instructed this morning on becoming a son of God is what it takes to get there. We must be peacemakers and emulate the very person of Jesus Christ before a world of division, hatred, competition and war. Jesus was not only giving instructions to His disciples and outlining what characteristics that their lives would take on, but He was also painting them a picture of Himself. As He always does, Jesus was sharing who He is so that they could learn from Him. Jesus was the ultimate peacemaker. His primary purpose was to make peace between God and man. He reconciled the world unto Himself. Everything else was first submitted unto that one thing.

So if we want to learn to be peacemakers, we must learn to give ourselves to others, just as Jesus did. That does not mean that we do this only through the means of instruction, preaching and teaching. It means that we must be willing to lay down our own lives for the benefit of others without consideration of their acceptance. Jesus died for us while we were still sinners. No conditions were made. All we have to do is have faith and receive. Therefore, this is our mandate before others. Give without condition. Love as Jesus loved. Serve as Jesus served. It is not easy and is defintely contrary to the ways of the world. But in doing so, we shall be called the sons and daughters of God.

Today's Prayer

Father, thank You so much for sending Your Son onto the earth. Thank You for calling men to His side that would write these accounts so that I can learn from them. I am amazed at how You still speak so clearly two thousand years after Your Son walked upon this earth. And through Your Word and witness of the Holy Spirit within me, I remain convinced that You still walk, live and breathe in my own heart! Man could not dream up a God like You! You are above and before all others! My heart is so comforted by simply knowing You. And my heart is convicted at the same time. My heart is pierced because I see how many times I am more concerned with being heard, or respected, instead of simply wanting to be completely reconciled to You. How many times have I complained to You instead of sitting at Your feet and learning? How many relationships have I done harm to because of my pride and insistence on being right? Forgive me Lord and help me to restore others unto me, just as You do. Help me to live in freedom by becoming a peacemaker. Teach me how to consider others' interests before my own. And in doing so, awaken my heart to the real blessings that await me through such a different lifestyle! Before You, in Jesus' name, and by the empowerment of the Holy Spirit, I pray these things, Amen!

Day Eight

On Heavenly Rewards

Today's Word

"Blessed are those who are persecuted for righteousness' sake, For theirs is the kingdom of heaven. Blessed are you when they revile and persecute you, and say all kinds of evil against you falsely for My sake. Rejoice and be exceedingly glad, for great is your reward in heaven, for so they persecuted the prophets who were before you." *Matthew 5:10-12*

Today's Thought

Today, we close out the Beatitudes. For sure, we haven't exhausted every conclusion we can gain by studying them, for the Bible is living and breathing. And it will speak just as much to you today and tomorrow as it has in the past. I encourage you to revisit the Beatitudes in the future, for they are truly the mandate of Jesus for Christians to be salt and light before the world. But as we close them out, let us remember that these instructions are the blessings of God. They are not to be reviled, as many Christians seem to think. They are meant for our growth and prosperity. So let's finish them up today with some real meat. Again, we must remember that our minds are warped to the natural world's training. And as people that have had personal experiences with Jesus, we have a distinct and desperate need to be retrained according to the principles of Heaven.

If we sum up the blessings that are noted in the verses above, it is possible to gain much perspective. Blessed are those that are persecuted, reviled, spoke evil against, and spoke falsely against. In our flesh, we scream out, "How can these people be blessed? The world hates them. Who is going to learn anything from someone they hate?" Again, if we try to understand this from a worldly perspective, we will lose any and all understanding and Kingdom perspective. We must remain firmly rooted in a Kingdom of Heaven mindset.

I see a gross atrocity going on within the Church today. We are being taught to accept everything in the name of tolerance. We are told that the Church must change with the times if we are going to be effective in the world around us. But that line of thinking is a polar opposite with the teachings of Jesus. Jesus wasn't worried about changing His message to fit the changing political and social documentary of His times. He simply lived transparently and obeyed the Father in all that was put before Him. And we must live likewise.

Now before we get too far into this idea of rebelliousness against the world, it is   very important to understand the methods by which we should do this. We are to be revolutionaries. But being revolutionaries only in the sense that we are sharing a message and doing things that others, who don't know Jesus personally, don't quite understand. We are not to be exclusive of the world. We are to be alive and well right in the midst of all the chaos around us. This is the life of a Christian. That has been the testimony of amazing followers of Jesus throughout the centuries. They stood for what was right in God's eyes, even if it cost them their own reputation. Are we supposed to escape such trials and struggles? Certainly not.

Jesus tells us here in *Matthew 5*, that we are actually blessed when we are hated because of our willingness to live out our beliefs in love and compassion. I add those last four words very intently- in love and compassion. We must always remember that we, too, were once lost and clueless. That keeps us from taking a stand in our own righteousness, or supposed "good works." There are plenty "Christians" out there who are standing up against immorality. Yet, there is no love or compassion in them. They have no understanding of what the true Gospel really is. It is loving those that hate you. It is considering it an honor when others speak falsely against you. And, it is being that witness of God's love, just as Jesus was. He laid down His life and resisted anger when others persecuted Him. Where are this type of Christians in our world?

It's easy to pick out the Westboro Baptist type of "Christians", and say that we're nothing like that. But what about seeing it in our own lives? Do we detest homosexuality so much that we hate those that live in it's lifestyle? Are we so angered by the atrocity of abortion that we don't cringe when we see others espousing our beliefs while being willing to hurt or hate others that have different viewpoints than our own? It seems, that in this era of declining growth of the Church, that we have lost our sense of purpose. We are called to lay down our own lives for a greater purpose. And in that process, we shall be blessed. The Gospel is meant for us- for you and I to be able to change our own lives. Let God do His job of growing the Church. If you want to know why church membership is down, know that it's probably ourselves that are in the way. When we learn to live in the demonstration of love, just as Jesus did, then and only then, shall we see a change.

Today's Prayer
Father, forgive me for my willingness to subscribe to the ideals of this world. You have called me to be an agent of change. You have called me to

align my own life to the principles that Jesus demonstrated. Yet, so often, I have quoted chapter and verse without allowing them to change me. I have looked for others to change while being unwilling to change myself. Forgive me Lord! I ask for You to inhabit this bodily dwelling fully. Encompass every expanse of my life. Fill me up with the Holy Spirit! Lord, help me to live appropriately before others. Help me see the blessings of life that You have outlined for me over the last week. And as I continue to study and learn from these words of Your Son Jesus, continue this beautiful process of change that is taking place within me. Break me from the world's mindset that has settled within me. Realign me to the life that You would have me live. Remove hate from my heart. Mold me as You see fit, regardless if others get it or not. I simply want to live purely before You. In Jesus' name, Amen!

Day Nine

Salt and Light

Today's Word

"You are the salt of the earth; but if the salt loses its flavor, how shall it be seasoned? It is then good for nothing but to be thrown out and trampled underfoot by men. You are the light of the world. A city that is set on a hill cannot be hidden. Nor do they light a lamp and put it under a basket, but on a lampstand, and it gives light to all who are in the house. Let your light so shine before men, that they may see your good works and glorify your Father in heaven." *Matthew 5:13-16*

Today's Thought

How many good for nothing Christians are running around in the world around me? Perhaps a better question is: "*How many days have I been a good for nothing Christian?*" Jesus makes some very strong comparisons here in the verses following the Beatitudes. We must not forget what we have just studied as we move into other concepts about the Christian life. Remember, that we are looking at three entire chapters of Matthew to find answers on how a Christian should be changed, or different from our old lives. And the Beatitudes serve as the foundation for this rebuilding of our lives. With Jesus as the cornerstone, we are putting principles into place that will cause us to live dramatically different lives.

When we lose our flavor, we become good for nothing. We are nothing more than a decoration. So, how does salt lose its' flavor? It becomes diluted with water. It is watered down, leaving the salt there but not as strong. This is the state of so many of our lives. We have been diluted with the philosophies and ideologies of the world, leaving us with a less than optimal impact. And looking into the words of Jesus, we see why the Church has such a minor impact on the world around us. We are thrown out and trampled under the feet of mankind.

But take heart! God loves the process of desalination. You see, the process of desalination removes water from the salt. Desalination separates salt from water so that water is good for drinking purposes. Thus, putting both salt and water into their original states. God wants to remove the impurities of the world from us. He does this through an intimate process of personal revelation. Through our willingness to submit all to Him, we will be renewed and made pure. And once purified, we can again be cast back out into the sea of humanity to flavor the world around us. By understanding this, we see the importance of drawing near to God daily. He makes me new again and again which keeps me useful for His purpose. This ties into the next idea of our light.

Jesus says that we are the light of the world. He does not say that we have the potential to be the light of the world, we **ARE** the light of the world. So when the world around us seems dim and dark, we need not look anywhere else but the mirror. I cannot change others, I can only change myself. Therefore, draw near to God once again. This is the continual plea of our Savior, "*Come to me all who labor and are heavy laden, and I will give you rest.*" - *Matthew 11:28* The early Church got this concept, for in *Acts 4:13* it says, "*Now when they saw the boldness of Peter and John, and perceived that they were uneducated and untrained men, they marveled. And they realized that they had been with Jesus.*" Although Jesus had resurrected some days before, Peter and John still walked in power and light because they spent their days with Jesus! Oh, what a beautiful testimony that awaits the Christian that is awakened to this truth!

Back into today's Word, Jesus then refers to Jerusalem, as Jerusalem is the city set on a hill. Jesus' first purpose was to enlighten the Jews. And to this day, all eyes remain fixed on Jerusalem looking for the light and the peace that only Jesus offers. All else is a cheap substitute.

But then, Jesus again makes it personal. This message is not just for the Jews that would choose to believe, but for all people that are willing to place their faith in Christ.

We are not to be hidden from the world. Like we talked about in the process of desalination, God draws us in, enlightens our hearts through intimacy with Him, and then sets us upon a lampstand so that others may be enlightened as well. He sets us apart. Theologians call this the process of sanctification. It means to be made holy. We are a royal priesthood, set apart from the world. And God's light shines from within us. Our good works are not fueled by our own efforts or our individual abilities. Rather, it is the light of God shining from within us. Our responsibility lies only in our willingness to draw near to Him. Think of yourself as a wick on a candle. We are lit when we draw near to the everlasting flame. The light we carry is not our own, it is the extension of God's light which has been shared with us.

As we move forward in this journey, let us keep in mind all that we have learned to this point. We are to be broken. Not out of fear or self-righteousness, but out of our willingness to submit because we see our need for God daily. Therefore, we draw close to Him. And when we draw close, He shares His purpose with us. He sanctifies us and purifies us. He then places us before the world to shine brightly so that others may experience the same goodness that we have experienced. He sets us before mankind as a witness of His love and continual warmth. His light within us is an invitation to those wandering in darkness. And our willingness to simply be open, transparent, and enlightened by God is all the world needs to be beckoned into this beautiful journey of faith with our Father.

Today's Prayer

Father, thank You for having a purpose for my life. So often, I have been watered down and I lose sight of Your purpose in my life. I know that You have placed me here, within this world at this specific moment in human history, for a reason. You do not make mistakes and Your timing is perfect. But so often Father, I get in the way of Your purpose and plan. So often, I make a mess of things. Forgive me Lord for not staying submissive in all I do. Forgive me for not drawing near to You and instead choosing to live in ignorance and fear. I truly know that like a flame which lights the candle, You simply seek to bring warmth and comfort to my soul and enlighten me so that I will no longer walk in darkness or fear. You are so compassionate and gentle with me Lord. I want to be more like You. Therefore, I walk into Your passionate embrace so that my life is filled with You. Holy Spirit, I give You free reign within this heart. Open my eyes so that I may see clearly and walk minute by minute within the grace that You offer. In Jesus' wonderful name, Amen!

Day Ten

Jesus, the Law and the Prophets

Today's Word

"Do not think that I came to destroy the Law or the Prophets. I did not come to destroy but to fulfill. For assuredly, I say to you, till heaven and earth pass away, one jot or one tittle will by no means pass from the law till all is fulfilled." Whoever therefore breaks one of the least of these commandments, and teaches men so, shall be called least in the kingdom of heaven; but whoever does and teaches them, he shall be called great in the kingdom of heaven. For I say to you, that unless your righteousness exceeds the righteousness of the scribes and Pharisees, you will by no means enter the kingdom of heaven." *Matthew 5:17-20*

Today's Thought

Jesus, in this beautiful discourse on proper living, might seem to take a strange turn here; but we need not be confused nor dismiss the importance of these words so quickly. Jesus is in the process of retraining the disciples. He has pulled them aside and is telling them about how man has misunderstood God for so long. The Righteousness that was demonstrated in the Law has turned into a sense of pride and self-righteousness. Where the Law had be given to set apart the Jewish people, certain Jews within the nation had twisted and manipulated the Law in order to gain control and become little gods between the people and God. This was never God's intent. And here is God in human flesh working the process of reconciliation between mankind and Himself.

Jesus says that He did not come to earth to destroy the Law, but to fulfill it. How important of a statement to make! In this one sentence, Jesus validates the entirety of the Old Testament. He makes the Old Testament applicable in each of our lives. There is so much history and applicable truth that we can learn from the Old Testament Word! Yet, so many Christians tend to ignore the Old Testament as something that doesn't really apply to us. We may read the Psalms and Proverbs, even occasionally dive into Genesis, but those Old Testament Prophets??? What do they have to do with our lives? The answer is ***everything***!

Jesus stated that He was purposed to fulfill the Law. He is saying that there is no need to look anywhere else but Him. Here, we see that the Law was never meant to be a decree of judgment over the inadequacies of mankind. It was meant to demonstrate that man could not be good enough independent from God. We need help. We need a mediator. Under the Old Covenant, a

High Priest entered into the Holiest of Holies to make amends between man and God. And Jesus is now comparing His Presence to the very presence of the High Priest! He is declaring Himself as the mediator between God and man! I am confident that the disciples' world was being shaken by every word Jesus is saying to them. All that they had ever been taught was being turned upside down. All that had made them feel so inadequate is being wiped away with every syllable from Jesus' lips.

The last couple of the verses that we are looking into today are very important as well. Jesus begins to set up how God intended the Law; as opposed to how man thought the Law was intended. The Law, whether it be the Levitical Law placed before the Israelites, or the Ten Commandments which were delivered from God's own hand, has only one purpose- to help man understand that we cannot be good enough on our own merits to obtain relationship with God. The Law is meant to show us that we must be fully dependent on God at all times.

Jesus fulfilled the Law by being fully dependent on the Father at all times. Fast forward to Jesus' discussions with the scribes and Pharisees. Whenever He was asked how and why He did the things He did, He always showed His dependence on the Father. Jesus refrained from sin by remaining so intimately close with Dad that His heart could not find a greater joy by any other means. This is the blessing of the Law. Growing in dependence is very different from growing independent. That is what the religious teachers had begun to do- grow independent from God. But Jesus continually demonstrated His full dependence on God.

Jesus also shares with the disciples the upcoming divide between the religious leaders of the day and Himself. When one begins to become independent from God, anything that threatens their position or power, threatens themselves. But if one is dependent on God and constantly intimate with Him, position and power have no value. Do you see the difference between Jesus and the scribes and Pharisees? One is seemingly self-righteous through illegitimate means and will therefore protect their territory at all costs. The other is justified by the Father Himself and therefore makes no boundary between Himself and others. One rules by fear and control and the other by love and compassion. This are the differences between God and man. And that's why man's way will never work.

I encourage you today, just as I encourage myself, to allow Jesus to continue to shake up your world. As He did with the disciples, let Him do with you. Allow God to have intimate connection with every ideology you've ever held. As we continue on in this teaching, which has become known as the Sermon on the Mount, ask God to give you complete understanding. Ask Him to make it real to you. This will change everything you are. It will break you from the mold of man and will allow you to submit to the full process of God. For what He did with the disciples 2,000 years ago, He also seeks to do with us.

Today's Prayer

Father, I am so thankful for Your instruction and guidance. Lord, You bless me with understanding and You invite me into true intimacy. I know that only my submission will allow me to obtain You fully. So I ask You in. Come deeper into my life than ever before. Help me see the constraints I have placed on You because of improper teaching and education. Lord, break all barriers that would keep me from experiencing You as fully as Jesus does. I am my Beloved's and He is mine! Lord, thank You for the promises and fulfillment of Your Word in the person of Jesus! Thank You for opening my eyes and calling me into relationship with You. For in You alone am I complete. Through You, I find the peace and joy that my heart craves! And in Jesus' wonderful name I declare, Amen!

Day Eleven

The Murderous Heart

Today's Word
"You have heard that it was said to those of old, 'You shall not murder, and whoever murders will be in danger of the judgment.' But I say to you that whoever is angry with his brother without a cause shall be in danger of the judgment. And whoever says to his brother, 'Raca!' shall be in danger of the council. But whoever says, 'You fool!' shall be in danger of hell fire." *Matthew 5:21-22*

Today's Thought
Before we even get into today's thought, we must remember that we are looking into one discourse of Jesus. In other words, we are building on all that we learned yesterday and Lord willing, tomorrow, we will build on the principles that we learn today. With that in mind, we remember that yesterday, we looked into how Jesus relates the Law to our lives. The Law is not our constraint, it is our guide and blessing. Therefore, I am excited to look into several of the laws that Jesus addresses.

Look at the first eleven words of the verses above. Jesus is addressing the traditions of man. Again, within just a few words, Jesus is challenging all that the disciples trusted because He is challenging the traditions of Israel. One of the most important things for us to pick up over the next several days is the new way Jesus is instructing. Over and over again throughout these referenced laws Jesus says, "*You have heard it..........but I say.*" He is again shaking the very foundations that religious life is based upon. He is addressing the heart. It's not about what others see, it's about what you know about yourself. When Jesus shakes our foundations, we will either stand obstinately firm, or we will allow our former selves to crumble so that we can be rebuilt according to His Word (*Matthew 21:42-44*).

Isn't it amazing that Jesus challenged the key paramounts of the Jewish faith? The most "righteous" of Jews prided themselves on their ability to stand in judgment over those that couldn't get the laws right. Paul even referred back to this when remembering that according to the Law he was perfect, but he was still as lost as a ball in high weeds. Christianity isn't about getting it right all the time. It's about being willing to be changed daily into the very image of Christ. It's about fulfilling the will of the Father. So when we see Jesus addressing murder here, we must understand where Jesus is going to take the discussion. He takes it where all of His discussions go- to the heart of mankind.

It's easy to say that I've never murdered someone. Very few people actually have. But do I hold hatred in my heart? Well, that's a totally different question. Jesus addresses the heart, which brings up the secret motives and desires that lie within all of us. Jesus says that whoever is angry without cause is in danger of the judgment. Well, what cause is justifiable? Can I excuse myself from these rigorous tenants of Jesus? If I realize just how much God has already forgiven me, then I have no authority to stand in judgment over anyone else. In other words, if I immediately question what is an acceptable anger and what is not, then I am missing the point all together. Our hearts should be penetrated and pierced just thinking about how many times we have lashed out at others in anger.

Jesus also uses a very interesting word here-Raca. Saying this in Jesus' time was basically saying that someone is good for nothing. Jesus equates anger to our judgment over others. Whether it be due to pride or just being judgmental, we must be aware of our heart condition at all times. Religious folks often think that the Ten Commandments are about our relationship with mankind. But it's more about our relationship with the Father. They are the calling of a loving God for our hearts.

When our hearts are right, we won't view others as good for nothing. God sees value in every life. How then can we judge others regardless of their sins? How can we view others as something less than ourselves? How can we have a greater value than others? We don't. And that's the point Jesus is making. He's saying don't be like the religious leaders who justify themselves by what others see. He's encouraging the disciples to go deeper with God. And that's a good place for all of us to go.

Today's Prayer
Father, thank You for giving me proper perspective today. Thank You for reminding me just how much You love others. So often, I become consumed with only my own interests. But today, You call me to be concerned with others as well. Help me to nurture the relationships that You have placed in my life. Whether it be a co-worker, my wife, my children, or just friends and acquaintances, I will not hide the light of the world that You have placed within me. I will shine brightly and You will be glorified. I will shine brightly because You purpose me to do so. Father, I give You continual permission to work on this hardened heart of mine. Even when I resist You, work Your love into me. I want to live in true freedom, just as Jesus did. And I know

that kind of life is found solely in You. Therefore, I submit. In Jesus' name, Amen!

Day Twelve

Be Reconciled

Today's Word

"Therefore if you bring your gift to the altar, and there remember that your brother has something against you, leave your gift there before the altar, and go your way. First be reconciled to your brother, and then come and offer your gift. Agree with your adversary quickly, while you are on the way with him, lest your adversary deliver you to the judge, the judge hand you over to the officer, and you be thrown into prison. Assuredly, I say to you, you will by no means get out of there till you have paid the last penny." *Matthew 5:23-26*

Today's Thought

As my pastor taught me early on in my Bible studies, any time you see the word "therefore", you must look back a verse or two and see what the verse you are looking at is "there for." So, remembering that yesterday we were talking about the importance of avoiding hate and discourse with our fellow man because that brings separation into your relationship with your Father, let's move into today's Word. Today, we see Jesus bringing up the idea of reconciliation and its' importance to our spiritual lives. So often, we think of our earthly relationships as something completely separate from our spiritual relationships. But Jesus states otherwise....

Look at how Jesus phrases the first verse above. If you are coming before God and remember that your brother has something against you, go and be reconciled so that you can approach God being clean. Perhaps it is stated differently in other places in the Bible, but I have always thought that this verse said that if we had anything against another, be reconciled first, then come before God. It is something entirely different for us to reconcile with someone that finds fault with us. Forgiving those that have wronged me seems a saintly thing to do. Therefore, it makes sense in my natural mind. But having to make up with those that are angry with me? Again, Jesus is shaking our foundational beliefs.

Why is it so important for us to seek reconciliation with someone that has division with us? Pride separates. Humility unites. These are *Kingdom Principles* that we must work into every aspect of our lives. A little pride will poison the entire well of our hearts. But being willing to cast down that pride by approaching those that have fault with us, this pierces our hearts. Let's make this a bit more practical.

Suppose my wife and I are fighting because she says that I haven't taken her on a date for too long of a period. Pride convinces me that she should see things from my perspective. After all, I'm doing all that I can as a husband and a father. I'm trying to divide my time appropriately between all the responsibilities that I have. I'm working hard and devoting time to her and the kids. Shouldn't she see how much I have on my plate? Therefore, I remain convinced that she is the one that needs to change, and I continue my spiritual journey thinking that all is well. But Jesus says otherwise.

Jesus says that I need to be reconciled or things will not be good between me and the Father. Why? Can I really control all that others think about me? Pride continues to encourage me that others need to change, not me. Pride tells me that I am right. And pride will keep me standing alone and not dependent on God. While it is true that I cannot control what others think about me, I can control what others see about my heart through my actions. And by my own seeking of forgiveness and reconciliation, I am demonstrating the very thing that Jesus did.

We must remember that Jesus came to earth, taught love and compassion, lived openly before others, and then died a sinner's death- all while we had not sought reconciliation with Him. He sought reconciliation with His very life. And in this, the Father was well pleased. When we seek out this type of living, we no longer crave the need to be justified by man. By seeking reconciliation with others, we are actually gaining reconciliation with God. We must always remember that Jesus was made evident as Lord by first becoming the servant of all. And into this service to others, we are called as well.

It is important that we should seek reconciliation at all times, even with our enemies. But we know that this is not always possible. For the same pride that so easily ensnares us also fills the hearts of our fellow man. But by demonstrating the principles that Jesus is teaching, we are demonstrating the love of God. And God is getting the glory. For others will see us operating by a different means. And they will truly recognize that as something more than just human.

So, what's more important to you and I today? Is it more important that others know we are right, or that we are right with God? By serving others and seeing reconciliation as more important than being right, we are taking on the attributes of God. Of course, as a disclaimer, I must state that evil is evil regardless of how it presents itself, so I'm not saying that we are to leave all of our convictions behind. But we can seek reconciliation without forgetting our principles. This is why Jesus demonstrated His love for three years before completing the act of reconciliation. In doing so, He continually demonstrated His love. His final act before humanity was to give His very life for those that actually hated Him. And, so often, I can't even find it in my heart to go an approach the ones that I have hurt. Proper perspective, huh?

Today's Prayer

Father, forgive me for remaining so prideful in my life. So often, I just think that it's everybody else that needs to change. But, You show me otherwise. You gently instruct me in the ways that my own heart needs to change. I thank You for that. Show me the relationships in my life that need mending. Help me to be Your light as I seek proper relationships with all those around me. Empower me beyond normal means. I love You, and I seek a proper relationship with You above all else. And I know that means that I must seek a proper relationship with others; even my enemies. But I don't know how to truly do that. So please help me in this. In Jesus' name, Amen!

Day Thirteen

The Adulterous Heart

Today's Word

"You have heard that it was said to those of old, 'You shall not commit adultery.' But I say to you that whoever looks at a woman to lust for her has already committed adultery with her in his heart. If your right eye causes you to sin, pluck it out and cast it from you; for it is more profitable for you that one of your members perish, than for your whole body to be cast into hell. And if your right hand causes you to sin, cut it off and cast it from you; for it is more profitable for you that one of your members perish, than for your whole body to be cast into hell." *Matthew 5:27-30*

Today's Thought

Oh, what a difficult saying this is for me to hear. For I recognize in myself the same need to be self-justified like the Pharisees of old. Jesus knew what men had taught for years, decades and perhaps centuries on the laws that God had put before them. Men, in their desire to be set apart and above others, made excuses for their sins by discounting them. Men say, "As long as we don't act on our thoughts, we're okay." Oh, what a cheapened way of living! And here is our Jesus, once again, tearing away all the stone walls of iniquity that have kept our hearts from truly experiencing a different way of living. Before you go any further today, know that my intent is not to embarrass, but to save. Therefore, consider these words and ask the Holy Spirit to give you understanding, the willingness to submit, and the true joy that follows obedience.

Jesus says, "*You have heard it said....but, I say.*" Know that the very One that delivered the Law to Moses is now instructing His followers on the intent of the Law. The Law is meant to expose our hearts before God so that we can be healed, not held- **no longer held** in contempt or imprisoned in our own sin. Jesus wants the inner man. For wherever the heart is, in that path the feet shall follow. David looked upon Bathsheba with lust before he sinned with her. And so, we get to the needed understanding of lust in mankind's heart. Let each of us learn and understand the importance of the Master's teaching.

Also, before we get too far into today's teaching, I must remind you several things about lust. Lust is coveting, another one of the Ten Commandments. While here we see lust referred to by Jesus in the context of adultery. Lust carries many forms. Perhaps you don't sexually lust, but do you lust for other things that the Lord has not delivered unto you? Do you lust for things? Do you desire someone else's husband?

Someone else's children? You see, all of these are forms of lust and cannot be discounted just because they are not explicitly spelled out by the Master. Again, we must remain fixed on the reality that Jesus is addressing the heart. Adam and Eve lusted for being equal with God and then consumed of the fruit of Knowledge of Good and Evil. Their sin was birthed within their hearts.

I used to struggle continually with lust. Finally, I reached a point of disgust with my own heart that I asked God for help. One day while praying, I asked God to help me see women differently. I asked Him to give me His eyes. I asked God to help me see the women before me as He saw them. And what God did with me was nothing short of a miracle. I started seeing women as daughters of the Almighty. Women stopped becoming objects of desire and I started seeing their hurts, wants and desires. I noticed that their flirtatious remarks toward me were often a voiced desire to be accepted and loved in a way that only God can accept and love. And that drove me to a deeper prayer life. There is nothing like looking at others and seeing them as God sees them!

Now before you start applying some form of sainthood upon me, I must confess that at times, I return to my former self. But now, by God's grace, I am able to recognize that if I am lusting, there is a disconnect between my heart and God. My eyes have turned to fleshly desires instead of spiritual cleanliness. And once again, God's kindness leads to my repentance. What a wonderful God we serve! So, I repent because I am reminded that I serving myself and not God.

So after we recognize that Jesus is concerned with our hearts, we must understand the seriousness of His instructions. Jesus says that if your eye or your hands cause you to sin, it is better for us to remove them from our bodies before we allow them to corrupt us to the point that we abandon our heavenly calling due to our sinful desires. This is serious talk. We must understand the importance of what Jesus is saying. For a little sin poisons the entire body. Therefore, submit all of your members to God. Don't try to keep one little sin for yourself and think it will be okay. Whatever sin holds your attraction or predisposition; if left unattended, or guarded from God, it will tear you away from Him. And it can easily ruin your entire life.

I believe that Jesus always words things carefully and with thoughtful intent. He first talks of the eye and then the hand. The eye implies desires, but the hand implies action. If we don't address the desire, action will follow. And if we don't address action, destruction shall follow. Do you get that? Think back to the reference of Adam and Eve that was brought up earlier. They first looked upon the fruit and saw that it was appealing. That fruit really looked good. The longer that they cast their eyes upon it, the less they were reminded that God had given them instruction to stay away from it. Finally, their desire led to action. They reached out their hands and plucked from the tree. And once they plucked from the tree, they bit into it. They took the fruit into their mouths and the fruit became part of them. Therefore, they devoured their own destruction. The desire led to action, which led to destruction. These words are the very same teaching that Jesus is sharing with us today. It is better to stop the desire than to taste the destruction. We must learn to recognize sin at its' earliest stages. And by doing so, we will experience the abundant life that only Jesus can offer us. May we all have the strength and submitted willingness to do.

Today's Prayer

My Gracious and loving Heavenly Father, thank You so much for delivering these words to me today. Thank You for speaking to my heart. I truly see that You love me too much to simply leave me the way I am. You seek the best for me, even better than I seek for myself. I so often feel like I have lost my way, and yet You continually remain beside me, calling me back into Your warm embrace. Thank You for not rejecting me as a sinner. Thank You for giving Yourself up and taking on my sin so that I can live forever with You. There is truly no God like You. You stand alone. God, I submit my heart to You today. For I know that if there is any one thing in my life that needs Your touch more than anything else, it is my heart. I ask for Your covering over my health, my finances, my work and my rest. But my heart I lay bare before You and ask that You provide true healing. In Jesus' name, Amen!

Day Fourteen

Jesus on Divorce

Today's Word
"Furthermore it has been said, 'Whoever divorces his wife, let him give her a certificate of divorce.' But I say to you that whoever divorces his wife for any reason except sexual immorality causes her to commit adultery; and whoever marries a woman who is divorced commits adultery."
Matthew 5:31-32

Today's Thought
What a contentious debate to get into these days....

I don't know if there is anything more volatile in today's culture than to discuss marriage and divorce. Homosexuals want the right to marry. Heterosexuals want to divorce without condemnation or attempts at reconciliation. So, we must look at the fullness of Jesus' teaching here in just a couple of verses. In order to fully understand, I feel we need to look into another passage where Jesus addresses marriage and divorce. So let's look at *Mark 10.*

The Pharisees came and asked Him, "Is it lawful for a man to divorce his wife?" testing Him. Mark 10:2

I encourage you to further study the next part of *Mark 10*, but let me clue you into just what's going on here. The Pharisees are testing Jesus, hoping to prove Him a heretic. Their only intent was to turn the people against Him and trip Him up. But in the full demonstration of God's graciousness and compassion, Jesus speaks to the heart of those hearing the conversation. You see, at the time of both the passage in Mark and the passage in Matthew, there were three schools of thought concerning marriage and divorce.

These ideas were promoted by three of the Jewish teachers, or Rabbis. Rabbi Shami taught that if a man married a woman and then found out on the wedding night that she was not a virgin, he was allowed to divorce her. Most people agreed with this teaching despite the fact that there was no way for a woman to prove she was a virgin. So, it was the man's word against the woman's word. Another school of thought was taught by Rabbi Hallel. He had a very liberal viewpoint of the Jewish Law regarding divorce. He taught that a wife was made unclean any time that her husband wasn't pleased with her. If she was too loud or too carefree in front of others, he could divorce her. If she didn't cook like he wanted, he could divorce her. Of course, men liked this ruling because it was meant to keep women in line and under the thumbs of their husbands. Next was a teaching by Rabbi Ocabe, who taught that if a man found a woman that pleased him more than his wife, he could justifiably divorce his wife. Isn't it funny that men will always twist and manipulate God's teachings in order to fulfill their own lustful desires?

So, posed with this trap, how does Jesus answer in *Mark 10*? He addresses the heart, which is where the problem really is. Jesus said in the verses following *Mark 10:2*, that the law was given to Moses because of the hardness of the people's hearts. Getting back to *Matthew 5*, we see that the only reason that Jesus says is acceptable for one to divorce another is because of sexual immorality, or adultery. But if we are to be forgiving and compassionate followers of Christ, is this alone reason enough? That's an individuals decision. But the Word makes it clear in *Malachi 2:16* that God hates divorce. Therefore, we must consider our actions well before committing them.

With these things in mind, how should we view our modern world in the context of Jesus' teachings? We know is that God does not change; so we must gain the understanding that it is not in our best interest to divorce. However, there are circumstances that make it justifiable. But again, we must always remember that this is an issue about our hearts. This is why a divorce rate of 50% within the Church is staggering and indicative of a Church out of touch with their Father.

Marriage is not easy, but it is sacred. The bond of marriage is more than just an earthly commitment. It is the completion of two souls becoming merged as one. It represents the relationship that God wants with each one of us. Therefore, when our hearts are willing to consider divorcing one another, we are so close, if not already in the place of divorcing ourselves from God. And our relationship with God is one that He will never break off. God says that He will never leave nor forsake us. It's not even in His vocabulary.

My life is not my own. When I asked Jesus into my life and accepted Him as Lord and Savior, He took my mess and made it clean. Then He said, *"Let me show you a better way to live."* This type of living is not easy nor is it for the faint of heart. But if we are willing to submit, oh what joy this type of living possesses! It changes us. And it causes us to think less about our own interests and more toward those around us.

The very same commitment lies at the core of every good marriage. It is two people living for the blessing of one another. And in this type of relationship, intimacy prevails. In this type of marriage, divorce is not an option. This is the heart of Jesus' teaching. Jesus wants us to view our marriages as something spiritual and a mirror image of our relationship with Him. When we are loving, patient and compassionate and our spouse is indifferent; instead of getting angry and frustrated, we must learn to turn to Jesus who is constantly loving toward us when we are indifferent. When we are forgiving, let us look to Jesus for proper guidance who forgave the entire debt of our sin towards Him. Now, this is the way I want to live.

Today's Prayer

Father, thank You for loving me consistently. Thank You for demonstrating the role of a faithful and loving spouse for me. When I comprehend how You love me, I truly realize that I don't have a clue as to how to love properly. So often, I have given in order to receive in return. I have loved so that I might be celebrated or appreciated. And I now know that that's not love at all. That's nothing more than pride disguised in a cheap facade of love. Father, forgive me. Continue to instruct me in the way I should go so that I will not depart from this blessed path on which You have set my feet. Lord, continue to mold my heart to Your own disposition. Open my eyes to greater truth and keep me from all iniquity. In Jesus' name, Amen!

Day Fifteen

Those Cursed Swear Words

Today's Word
"Again you have heard that it was said to those of old, 'You shall not swear falsely, but shall perform your oaths to the Lord.' But I say to you, do not swear at all: neither by heaven, for it is God's throne; nor by the earth, for it is His footstool; nor by Jerusalem, for it is the city of the great King. Nor shall you swear by your head, because you cannot make one hair white or black. But let your 'Yes' be 'Yes,' and your 'No,' 'No.' For whatever is more than these is from the evil one." *Matthew 5:33-37*

Today's Thought
Again we see Jesus shaking the very foundations that His followers had thought were law. As we continue this journey through the Sermon on the Mount, I am reminded of the prophet Jeremiah's words when God spoke through him, "*I will put My law in their minds and write it on their hearts....*" Here is Jesus penetrating the hearts of His new followers. He is writing His law as it should be- with grace on their hearts! And, He chooses His words wisely so that there can be no misinterpretation. Let each of us hear what God is saying and consider well how we use those old curse words.

Being a son of the South who was brought up in traditional ways, I was taught early on to watch what I say and to stay away from all of those filthy four letter words. And while those four letter words may demonstrate ignorance, they will certainly not send us to Hell. The swear words that Jesus is talking about here is nothing more and nothing less than talking out of turn. That's basically what matters. Who decides the entirety of our days? Who fills the voids of our moments with blessings unknown? It is none other than God Himself. Why then, should we be so sure of our days? This is what Jesus is communicating.

We swear things to others because they distrust us. If I tell someone that I'm going to do something, and I or someone else has not followed through in the past, then they will be looking for further assurance. I have noticed, through personal observation, that when I am going through difficult times, I want further assurances. A simple yes and no doesn't seem to be enough. Faith seems difficult because it is where the rubber meets the road.

But Jesus wants us to live like Himself, fully dependent on God at every moment. If we live this way, we will demonstrate our faith openly. Just a few verses before this, Jesus told the disciples to let their light shine before all of mankind. Now, He is giving them practical application. Stay away from hate, be reconciled with others, don't lust, stay true to those around you while allowing God to use them to grow and mature us, and don't make promises you can't keep.

As I continue on in my journey with Christ, I am realizing that moment by moment I need to keep my eyes fixed on Him. In this walk, I'm always watching for His guidance. I'm turning at the utterance of His voice. And in this new way of living, I am content. I want to make assurances to others, but I have to first go check with my Father. What if we all lived this way? What if instead of making hopeful promises to others without really knowing what God's will is in the given situation, I simply say, "Lord willing, we will do so." I'm learning to live like this and by doing so I know that wherever He leads me, I will be secure and confident that I am right where I need to be.

Today's Prayer
Father, You bless me beyond belief. You raise me up and take me to heights that I could never imagine! You bring understanding to my simple mind. And You bring blessings my way through every second of every day. Lord, I submit freely to You. I will look for Your guidance and instruction in all things. By Your grace alone, I will

not swear and will not falter. Lord, thank you for all that You are and for all You have done. I look forward to the days ahead!   In Jesus' name, Amen!

Day Sixteen

Turn the Other Cheek

Today's Word
"You have heard that it was said, 'An eye for an eye and a tooth for a tooth.' But I tell you not to resist an evil person. But whoever slaps you on your right cheek, turn the other to him also."
Matthew 5:38-39

Today's Thought
All of Jesus' teachings are equally important, so we dare not highlight one over any other. However, there are times in human history when there seems to be a propensity within society to really need to hear one truth.   And I think that these two verses are hugely important within today's society. Just this morning, I was reading about how Coptic Christians are under tremendous persecution in Egypt since the recent outing of Morsi.   Seven Christians have been killed recently in Egypt just because they were identified as Christians. In America, there seems to be a growing intolerance towards Christians. Therefore, let us heed well the instructions of our Master during these tumultuous times.

We know that the Law was given to the Children of Israel as a guide for how they should live their lives. We also know that Jesus was the fulfillment of the entirety of the Law. And so, if we, like the Israelites, seek to fulfill the Law ourselves, we must align our lives to the teachings of Jesus. Jesus speaks some very hard truths here that we must each be willing to accept. Do not repay evil with evil, but turn the other cheek. Sounds good theoretically, but how will we really respond when it is time to put it into action? Well, let's consider the life of Jesus. Particularly, the last few days of His life.

Jesus sat and dined at the table with the very man that would betray Him and offer Him up to be crucified. Being all powerful and all knowing, Jesus withheld the fullness of this truth from the disciples. I'm sure that if a roughneck like Peter would have known what Judas was planning, he would have taken Judas out himself. So even in the withholding of information, Jesus was demonstrating turning the other cheek. Also, Jesus could have taken Judas out Himself. But instead, Jesus submitted to the will of the Father, which was for the good of all mankind and not just Jesus, so He turned the other cheek.

Think also of how Jesus responded when brought before Pontius Pilate. The chief elders and leaders of the Jews were accusing Jesus of many things. And there Jesus stood remaining silent. Pilate even asked Jesus if He heard all that He was being accused of. And Pilate marveled because Jesus remained silent. In this moment, Jesus could speak the truth of God about Himself that would have humbled all. But He saw the will of the Father as something more important that being justified before man.

This brings me to the reality of what an "eye for an eye" truly entails. While most will quote this and declare it is justice. It is equally about being justified. I want others to know that they are wrong and I am right. That's the heart of the issue. You see, when I realize all that I am guilty of before God, and yet, He forgives me, clothes me in His Righteousness and calls me His own son. In fact, He declares me to be a co-heir with the very Son that I for so long rejected and cried out for His death! How then, can I place myself in a position of judgment over another fellow sinner and say that they should have to pay for the wrongs they've committed? Should I not have to pay for the very wrongs I've committed? Instead of crying out for justice, our hearts should be broken to where we cry out "Mercy!"

I share this today realizing that this is a work that we may have to work through our entire lives in order to be fully completed. I think of this being one of the first teachings of Jesus to His new disciples and then I quickly remember Peter cutting off an ear of one of the guards that came to arrest Jesus in the Garden of Gethsemane.

Jesus quickly replaced the soldier's ear and withheld Peter's hand from further violence. In this, Jesus was turning the other cheek. Jesus healed one of the very men whose sole purpose was to destroy Him. And in this same way of life, we are called to live.

Most of the time that I see others crying out for justice, it is because they possess a lack of trust in the Father. We must always remember that not one sparrow falls to its death without the Father taking notice. He has every hair on our heads numbered. We are God's prized possession! He knows all about us. Do we not trust Him to guide us through the dry places of life? Can He not accomplish His will through us, even when we are brought into the most dire circumstances? The life of a true follower of Christ is not promised to be an easy road, but it is a blessed road. The problem with most of us is that we consider God's blessings of material possessions and life itself to be greater than the real blessing of God- that He chooses to call us friends and that He longs to have a real and intimate relationship with us. Things can never equal relationship. And as long as our perspective is off in this, we will probably continue to quote the Law instead of fulfilling it. But that's not the life we are called to live.

Today's Prayer

Father, so often, I have cried out to You for justice. Forgive me for that. For I know that if I am willing to cry out for justice, I must be wiling to accept justice for my own sins. Lord, I ask for mercy over my sins. Therefore, I ask for mercy over the sins of others. I need You to complete this work in me. Help me as I seek to honor You and accept the hard aspects of the Christian life that seem so against my own prosperity. I know that when my flesh is stronger than my Spirit, that I will question difficult times, however they present themselves. I simply long to have the trust in You that allows me to endure the greatest adverse circumstances with grace and the purity of Jesus. Help me in the areas where I am so weak. I pray these things confidently, knowing that You hear me, and knowing that You will receive glory as I live as Jesus lived. I will keep my eyes on You Father. For within the embrace of Your arms is the only place where I find the peace that my soul so desperately longs for. In Jesus' name, Amen!

Day Seventeen

Give and Trust

Today's Word
"If anyone wants to sue you and take away your tunic, let him have your cloak also. And whoever compels you to go one mile, go with him two. Give to him who asks you, and from him who wants to borrow from you do not turn away."
Matthew 5:40-42

Today's Thought
To quote one of my dear friends who replies back to these devotionals regularly, "Ouch. Hallelujah!" Today's Word really hits home to me. Just when I think that Jesus can't dig any deeper into my heart, He uncovers soil that has been undisturbed for quite some time. So much time, in fact, that it is hardened. And yet, here is the gentle touch of my Master, tearing apart every inch of solidity which I have based so much of my life upon.

Yesterday, we talked on justice. And yesterday, the Good Lord showed me that rather than crying to the Lord "Justice!" when I am wronged, my heart should be in the place to beg for mercy. And this morning, Jesus says to put this into action. I must learn what submission truly is. And if I am unwilling to fully submit, I must be able to recognize where the problem really lies. If I am unwilling to let go, then I am seeing all of my possessions as mine as opposed to me simply being the steward over what God has placed in my life. Let me explain.

Jesus says that if someone asks you for your coat, give to him your shirt as well. How backwards does that seem in a world that continually teaches us to hold tightly to what we've worked so hard for? It's one thing to give to someone because they ask you, but if they sue you, give them more than what they're asking for! Why would He say such things? How does that even seem right? It's right because it exposes the true position of our hearts. And that's what Jesus is after- that and nothing more.

If I am willing to give until it hurts, even to those that don't deserve it; then I am beginning to step into the love that God has for all of mankind. Life is not about stuff- it's about loving God and loving others. The more that I love God, the more I will trust God. The more I trust God, the more I am able to learn from God. And the more I learn from God, the more I will begin to love others....even more than myself. You see, as long as we live in a place where we feel we must be justified at all times, we will never experience the fullness of God. The fullness of God is found by emptying ourselves out. We must become like Jesus, a drink offering for saints and sinners alike.

The second issue that Jesus is addressing here is what I alluded to earlier. There is a distinct difference between being owners and being stewards. If we can welcome the idea of stewardship into our lives, we are on our way to true freedom. You see, all the stuff that we possess is really just borrowed. God entrusts it to us. We are meant to simply take care of the things God has given us the pleasure to obtain. But once we step into the realm of possessing things, we will surely find out that it is actually we that are possessed by those things. They will become nothing more than a curse. And our lives will be cursed because of them.

When we take on this idea of stewardship, we are no longer bound to jealousy or covetousness. We realize that we have what we have because it is God's will. The man that has many possessions around him has a greater difficulty in welcoming the responsibility of stewardship. This is what Jesus addressed in *Matthew 19* when He said that it is easier for a camel to enter through the eye of a needle than for a rich man to enter heaven. It is not impossible. But the wealthy man better have a right understanding of stewardship, or he will lose out on the greatest riches that this world and the next has to offer!

Allow me to close today's devotional with this thought. I love the fact that Jesus puts this teaching into very simple terms with very small items- coats and shirts, walking the extra mile, and not turning away those that ask from you. You see, these are things that all of us have in common. In other words, the responsibility of stewardship and the freedom of the abundant life is equal for all of us. Whether you are a millionaire, or you just simply have enough to pay the bills every time they come due, we are all in the same position. Will we give with mercy in mind? Or, will we reject the teachings of our Master and hold tightly onto all that we have worked our lives to obtain? Make no mistake about it. The choice we make in these circumstances have two very different outcomes. One brings blessing and life. The other brings curses and death. So what are you moved to do?

Today's Prayer
Father, I am amazed at how You lovingly humble me day after day. You speak to my heart and uncover areas that need Your loving touch. Thank You for being so kind and gentle with me. I am truly in awe of Your Word and Your willingness to move in my heart. For so long, I have been just like the thief on the cross beside Your Son demanding that He get us out of this situation. All the while, You patiently wait with Your hand extended towards me offering me a better way of

living. And even though circumstances may be painful, the gift that You offer supersedes anything that this world could offer in the immediate. So, my sweet God, my Abba and my All, invade this life of mine and make it a sweet incense before Your throne! Saturate me with Your goodness and Your love. Thank You for Your continual instruction. For I know that in Your chastening, I am loved tremendously. I truly long for nothing but You. Forgive me for asking or expecting anything else that is actually nothing but a cheap counterfeit of that which I truly desire- that I may live in Your Presence for the rest of my days. Fulfill this prayer in me. In Jesus' most gentle name, Amen!

Day Eighteen

Loving Others Like Rain

Today's Word

"You have heard that it was said, 'You shall love your neighbor and hate your enemy.' But I say to you, love your enemies, bless those who curse you, do good to those who hate you, and pray for those who spitefully use you and persecute you, that you may be sons of your Father in heaven; for He makes His sun rise on the evil and on the good, and sends rain on the just and on the unjust. For if you love those who love you, what reward have you? Do not even the tax collectors do the same? And if you greet your brethren only, what do you do more than others? Do not even the tax collectors do so? Therefore you shall be perfect, just as your Father in heaven is perfect."
Matthew 5:43-48

Today's Thought

Today, we close out these moments of Jesus defining the Law as it should be. This is the sixth statement that contrasts God's ways against what the religious teachers have been teaching for so long- *"You have heard it said......but I say...."* Jesus has just taught us the last five of the Ten Commandments from *Exodus 20* as they were meant to be learned. The first five commandments deal with us as individuals and the individual choices that we make. The last five Commandments have to deal with how we relate to others. They are our divine moral code before the world. So, did Jesus just leave out the first five or did He completely forget about them? I believe that Jesus stayed away from the first five Commandments because they tell us how we are to live before God in order to live a blessed life. Over the next three and a half years of ministry, they would be brought up and addressed. Jesus is our demonstration and therefore, His heart says, let me show You how I live before the Father in order to live the blessed life. But then He tells us how to live before others. With that understanding, let us continue on.

We know that we are supposed to love our neighbors. Jesus flips the script here in that He shows something completely different. We are supposed to love our enemies. We are supposed to pray for those that come against us. How often within our beloved faith have we seen Christians pray against our enemies? How often have I sought out God only to request Him to smite down those that are coming against me? When something or someone hurts us deeply, we can be tempted to run to God and ask Him to make everything better. And He is willing to make everything better. However, that often comes through the process of our own pain and suffering. Jesus is not our Divine Bodyguard. We must always remember that He is after our hearts. And we are to live contrary to the rest of the world.

In fact, Jesus even references the ways of the world in the verses above. He says that the world greets their brethren happily and loves those that are like themselves. However, Jesus calls us to live more deeply. We are called to love those that hate us. I don't know about you, but I am fully confident that I cannot do that by my own strength. In the past, when others have sought out my destruction, I wanted revenge. I wanted God to show them that He was boss. And I wanted Him to come to my rescue. And sure enough, He came to my rescue. But He came to rescue my heart from anger and bitterness. And when things didn't turn out like I thought they should, I questioned God as to where He was in the midst of my turmoil and despair. The truth is that I couldn't see Him because I was looking for Him to be on the other side of the fence destroying my enemy. But He was right beside me hoping I would allow Him to continue His work within me.

There are two things that Jesus says in the verses above to which we should pay close attention. He says, "*..that you may be sons of your Father in heaven*" and "*Therefore you shall be perfect, just as your Father in heaven is* *perfect.*"   Jesus is sharing with us why these tenets of the Christian faith are so important. For within the words of Jesus, we find relationship and completeness. Jesus has just stripped away how man has related to the Law for centuries. He is sharing and demonstrating a new way of living that brings us into such intimate relationship with the Father that we are called sons. Jesus says, *"If you want to be perfect like the teachers of your days claim to be, work on these things. Let me have your heart."*

Lastly, we must realize why Jesus is sharing these things.   He is sharing these teachings because these teachings reveal the heart and character of God.   We are not called to be different just for the sake of being different. We are called to be like Dad. Jesus says that the Father causes the sun to rise and the rain to fall on both the evil and the good alike. God shows no partiality. Neither should we. For if we deal with friends and enemies differently, how can we expect to ever demonstrate the love of God before an unbelieving world?

Jesus started this discourse with the blessings of living life as we should and redefining the terms of success for the Christian life. Then He called us to be salt and light before the world. Just as Jesus stepped down from His heavenly throne and entered a world of sin and despair for our salvation alone, we likewise must follow suit. Once, we become a follower of Christ by faith, our heavenly citizenship is made complete. Yet, He calls us to live like He did. Remain among the rest of the world that is still without faith. Be salt and light. Preserve others and show them the way. And by doing so, we will start to demonstrate the Father before the rest of the world. That is what makes us co-heirs with Christ. That is what God's will is for each of our lives. Live differently, and live with intention and purpose. By doing so, not only will our own lives be changed, but God uses us to change those around us as well. What an amazing God we serve!

Today's Prayer

Father, thank You for opening up Your Word to my heart this day. Lord, You cause me to view my life differently. You ask me to allow You to enter in so that I can be made into something more. Lord, I am willing. Forgive me for my sins against my brothers and sisters of this world. Forgive me for my bitterness and continual cries for justice. Help me desire mercy. Show mercy to those that have dealt harshly with me in the past. Demonstrate love to those that are lost and without a vibrant relationship with You. And by Your empowering Holy Spirit, I will serve as evidence of that love and mercy. Lead me in the way I should walk before others. And keep me from simply putting up a front and pretending to be different. I need You to change this heart of mine so that I am completely different. Lord, I seek Your will above all else, for I know that Your plans are to prosper me, to give me a future and a hope. Use me as salt and light so that others may see how completely good and loving You are! Set my life afire with Your love, compassion, mercy and tenderness! In Jesus' wonderful name, Amen!

Day Nineteen

Being Charitable

Today's Word
"Take heed that you do not do your charitable deeds before men, to be seen by them. Otherwise you have no reward from your Father in heaven. Therefore, when you do a charitable deed, do not sound a trumpet before you as the hypocrites do in the synagogues and in the streets, that they may have glory from men. Assuredly, I say to you, they have their reward. But when you do a charitable deed, do not let your left hand know what your right hand is doing, that your charitable deed may be in secret; and your Father who sees in secret will Himself reward you openly." *Matthew 6:1-4*

Today's Thought
Interesting concept that Jesus is bringing to our attention today. We must not forget where we were yesterday, for in our message yesterday, Jesus told us to do good to all men. And today, we are reminded to not do good before men. Again, we see that Jesus is after our hearts. Picture Jesus within this intimate setting, teaching to those closest to Him. They are gathered together away from the crowd. And He is training them how to live a new life. He is teaching them, and us, that we must live contrary to the world.

The world lives according to the flesh, but we are called to live according to the Spirit. Therefore, we should do good to all men *but before no men*. Do we trust God enough to keep our good works secret?

What's more important to you, earthly rewards or heavenly rewards? You see, as friends of God and co-heirs with Jesus, God will withhold no good thing from us if we live according to the Spirit. For if God rewarded us when we live according to the flesh, He would be untrustworthy. But He's not. He's the most trustworthy thing or being that there is. And God, who is trustworthy and secure, says for you and I to do good to others when no one else can see. In fact, we are to keep it so secret that we keep our left hand does not even know what our right hand is doing. In other words, don't even acknowledge the kindness that you are showing to others within yourself.

For the second that the proverbial cat is out of the bag is the very second that we have received our reward. It's in our nature to be good to those like ourselves. But yesterday Jesus challenged us to be good to all men, even those that are not good to you. That's against our nature. It's in our nature for us to want to brag on the good things we do. We brag on our kids. We brag on our spouses. And especially when we're feeling insecure in any way, we will begin to brag on our ourselves. But Jesus says for you and I to fight that nature. Fight that necessity to be justified by man and choose to be justified by God.

As I contemplate this teaching of Jesus, I am reminded of the many times that Jesus instructed others to keep secret the good work or miracle that He had performed for them. I used to think that it was because Jesus didn't want His glory to be made known to those who were not ready to see it. But after reading today's passage, I think that Jesus simply did not want to be robbed of the rewards of His Father. Jesus' reward was for Him to continue to do the good works that His heart enjoyed. At some point, Jesus must have surely known that His glory would be so evident all around Him that He needed it kept quiet. For once His glory had become known to all, man would surely want to squash it. Jesus wanted things kept quiet because of His love for us. The longer the whole of society remained in the dark, the longer He could stay and continue to serve. But once His power rose to the level of a major threat to those in power, they would not wait any longer to remove Him.

I am also reminded of how Jesus dressed compared to all of the religious leaders of His day. You see, Jesus looked like everyone around Him. It was the priests and teachers that wandered the streets in fine clothing of bright colors. Everyone noticed everything that those people did. When they stopped to bless a crippled person on the side of the road, everyone said, "Oh, what a wonderful thing to do! He took time out of his busy schedule to pray with a needy person." But this was not so with Jesus. He blended in. Not only did God camouflage Himself in humanity, but He camouflaged Himself within humanity. Oh, how desperate of a people we are. We constantly crave attention. But not so with God. At His heart, He simply longs to bless. He makes Himself of no reputation so that He can move freely in blessing. What if you and I were to walk in the same manner? Oh, the rewards that surely would await us!

As I close out today's devotional, I am forced to ask myself, "Would I rather receive glory from God or glory from man?" Without a doubt, the answer is surely God. My problem is that when I do things openly before others, it is because I don't trust God to fulfill my need of being appreciated. But if, in my heart, I know that God fulfills my every need and that He is trustworthy, I will not fear being unnoticed. I will welcome it, knowing that my Heavenly Father takes notice of all things. That kind of thinking changes my heart. And it makes me more like my Master. Could I really ask for a greater reward?

Today's Prayer

Father, thank You for opening my blind eyes to such glorious truth. Lord, help me live an unnoticed life so that the rewards from Your mouth will overflow my life. When others do take notice, help me to be like Your Son who always gave recognition to You. Through understanding, I can now begin to see that You choose to receive glory over man because You alone can handle the recognition. You instruct me to not place myself in the acknowledgement of men because You know that I cannot handle it. Forgive me for being such a prideful man. So often, I brag on myself because I want others to say that I am a good man. How foolish I have been! Lord, I simply want to be acknowledged by You. Reward me as You see fit, for I truly know that within Your blessing is more joy than I can even contain. Lord, thank You for equipping me with Your Word so that I can fight my own sinful nature. Help me to look only to Jesus who is that author and finisher of my faith. I want to keep my eyes on You at all times and in all circumstances. I am blessed simply by being Your Son. In Jesus' name, Amen!

Day Twenty

When You Pray

Today's Word

"And when you pray, you shall not be like the hypocrites. For they love to pray standing in the synagogues and on the corners of the streets, that they may be seen by men. Assuredly, I say to you, they have their reward. But you, when you pray, go into your room, and when you have shut your door, pray to your Father who is in the secret place; and your Father who sees in secret will reward you openly. And when you pray, do not use vain repetitions as the heathen do. For they think that they will be heard for their many words. Therefore do not be like them. For your Father knows the things you have need of before you ask Him." *Matthew 6:5-8*

Today's Thought

It is interesting to me how Jesus describes prayer along the same lines as our charitable deeds. For they are both an act of goodness which must be inspired by God in order to have any real and lasting effect. Prayer is a gift from God. It allows us to truly commune with the Creator of the universe who also is the very Creator of our souls. It is time for intimate relationship between man and God. And so, Jesus clearly defines the difference between prayer and the act of prayer in two distinct ways: prayer is personal and intimate while the act of prayer is meant for personal glory and gain.

Although we have been studying the last chapter of Matthew over several weeks, we cannot forget that this is one passage directed to the disciples at the beginning of their walk with Jesus. He is instructing them that they must beware of the Pharisees. Surely, there were some good hearted Pharisees in the lot, but the majority of religious leaders were poisoned by their own self-glorification. What an important lesson for pastors, leaders, and the rest of the flock within today's Church to take note of! *"Beware of the leaven of the Pharisees and Sadducees...."* These are the words Jesus spoke in *Matthew 16*. And they are as applicable today as they were two-thousand years ago.

Why would Jesus warn the disciples about the Pharisees and speak so intently against them? It is because our hearts are naturally drawn to success. And surely, these men of faith that have so much power and that so many respect must be blessed by God. But Jesus tells us otherwise. Our greatest success is found in the secret places of our lives. For within those secret and intimate moments, we find true relationship with the persons of Father, Son and Holy Spirit. Jesus is letting us in on the secret that so many have longed and sought for thousands of years! The path to purpose, fulfillment and wonder in our lives is not a public journey- it is the intimate and individual walk with the Creator.

Jesus also instructs us on the true way to pray. God already knows all the intimate details of our lives. We do not have to fill Him in on everything. We simply need to approach Him with sincerity of heart and ask all that we need. One may ask why we even need to pray if God already knows all the things we need. Jesus addressed this in *John 15:16* when He said *"that whatever you shall ask of the Father in my name, He may give to you."* Jesus is relating the heart of the Father. Sure, God knows everything that we need; but His desire is that we would join in the process of obtaining our needs. We each have a choice as to whether to ask God for our needs, or to strive to obtain them through our own efforts. Submission brings us closer to God, whereas independence separates us from Him.

Prayer is truly submission of the heart. It cannot be overlooked nor its' importance minimized in the believer's walk with God. It is not about what we say, it is about the heart that says it. It is not about the eloquence of our words, but about the sincerity of our heart. One of my favorite prayers within the Bible is only but two words. Peter, after taking his eyes off of Jesus, simply cried out

"Save me!" and the Lord quickly came to the rescue. Do you get it? If so, then get to it.

Today's Prayer

Father, thank You for caring so much for us that You instruct us on how to communicate with You. You show me over and over again that You care for me! Oh, how You care for me! I am overwhelmed by Your love! Lord, help me to keep myself free from the trappings of this world and to always submit myself to You. Keep me from being impressed by my prayers. I simply long to know You more! Bless me as You see fit and as You know what is best for me. Thank You for providing daily all that I need to be complete in You and for empowering me to be effective in my testimony of You. I submit myself to You this day. In Jesus' name, Amen!

Day Twenty-One

Praying Like Jesus

Today's Word
"In this manner, therefore, pray: Our Father in heaven, Hallowed be Your name." *Matthew 6:9*

Today's Thought
I must start out today's devotional giving due credit to Robert Morris of Gateway Church. I have been so excited getting to this point in Jesus' Sermon on the Mount. And much of the reason for that excitement is because I have literally been saturated in learning how to pray through a teaching that Robert Morris did entitled *The Lord's Prayer*. I encourage you that if your heart is touched in some way by this devotional, or the devotionals in days to come, then look up Gateway Church and order that series.

Jesus is talking intimately with His disciples. And through the power of the Living Word of God, the Holy Spirit chooses to intimately communicate this with you and I as we begin to understand the real purpose of prayer. I truly believe that so many Christians remain mostly ineffective in their spiritual witness because we struggle with understanding just how important prayer is in our lives. Jesus just finished telling the disciples how they should pray, and now He actually demonstrates a true prayer. It is important to note that there is always power in demonstration. As Christians, our lives are to be demonstrative. We are the witness of Christ's love before a needy world. Therefore, let this word soak deep within your spirit today and begin to exercise spiritual strength in prayer.

Notice that Jesus starts by saying "In this manner..." He doesn't say, "Pray these words." Have you ever noticed that some individuals pray the same prayer over and over again? We must learn that praying is nothing more than having conversation with God. If I said the same thing to you every time we had a conversation, then our relationship wouldn't grow much. In fact, you'd probably avoid me. Thankfully, God promises to never leave nor forsake us. But, if we want our relationship with God to grow, we must learn to communicate with God properly. Pray like this. Remember, Jesus had just said that people that think that God will hear them due to their many words or vain repetitions are sadly mistaken. God simply wants to hear from our heart.

Speaking intimately, Jesus says, *"Our Father...."* What a beautiful and powerful statement these two words make! Jesus is inviting us into the very same relationship that He has with God. He is telling us that God wants to have the very same relationship with us that Jehovah has with Him.

God is our Father. Now there are two spiritual fathers which all men choose to serve. Either we will buy into the deceptions of Satan and serve him, who is the father of lies; or we will submit our will and hearts to God and serve Him, who is the Father of Lights. Make no mistake about it, we all serve someone. And if we choose to simply serve ourselves, we are truly deceived by Satan. For that is the very same thing that he choose to do.

Then Jesus adds the words "..*who art in Heaven, Hallowed be Your name.*" The very Creator of the universe, the God who knit together our souls while we were still within our mother's wombs, desires to have an intimate relationship with you and I! This truly sounds too good to be true! But in God's compassion and love for mankind, it is the only thing He longs for. God simply wants you and I to jump into His lap and talk to Him, our Daddy. He seeks to love and oversee us like no one else can. He seeks our hearts so that He can cultivate them and secure them. He does not want sacrifice, He wants to share His mercy with us!

I entitled today's devotional *Praying Like Jesus* because in the few words which start what has become known as *The Lord's Prayer*, we find a sweet invitation of intimacy from Jesus who is communicating the heart of our Heavenly Father.

And with that in mind, let us look forward to what the Holy Spirit will communicate to our hearts over the next few days. When we pray, we must always remember that we are speaking to God the Father, through the power and leading of the Holy Spirit, in the name and likeness of Jesus Christ. The fullness of the triune presence of God should be experienced in each and every time that we open our mouths to pray. Therefore, let us pray.

Today's Prayer
Our Father, thank You for inviting us into Your Presence today. Thank You for sending Your Son and empowering Him through the Holy Spirit so that our hearts may be enlightened and so that we can experience the fullness of Your love in every moment of our days! Lord, You truly amaze me with Your sweetness. I so often hold back from You, but You never hold back from me! You offer intimacy with You with every breath I breathe! Thank You! Empower me today, just as You empowered Your Son, so that I may be the light of the world. Lord, You are the Father of Lights. You are my Father, my Abba, my Daddy. I submit myself to You and sit at Your feet today, simply longing to be fully loved and instructed well. Have Your way with me. In Jesus' name, Amen!

Day Twenty-Two

Kingdom Come

Today's Word
"Your kingdom come. Your will be done on earth as it is in heaven." *Matthew 6:10*

Today's Thought
Yesterday, we talked on the invitation of prayer. Prayer is first an invitation extended to us from God. He desires our communion with Him. How glorious is that? But, the invitation is truly bilateral. For once we accept God's invitation of intimacy, Jesus instructs us to extend the offer back to Him. So, we are supposed to invite God's kingdom on earth? What does that even mean?

We are to learn to accept God's will for our lives. God's will is that no one should perish. Therefore, through our continued submission, God will put us in places and use our lives to reach others. Think of it this way- If God chose to use the form of a man, in the person of Jesus, in order to save mankind, why would He use any other means for mankind to be continually saved? You see, it is the continued witness of mankind that God uses to share His most intimate love. It is a changed life that changes other lives. That is at the heart of the Gospel. So prayer is an invitation into intimacy and an acceptance of submission.

I spent many years trying to figure out what God's will was for me. All the while, I was already living it. If you're anything like me, you've probably wondered many times when things are all going to line up and seem like all is well. All I can tell you from my personal experience is that on this side of Heaven, *they never will*. You see, if I am ever able to get truly comfortable here on earth, then this will be recognized as home within my heart. But it's not my home. It is a land strange and curious to my soul. Heaven is my home. I am just an alien and a pilgrim passing through. My goal then, is to get others to join me in my journey home.

So, this invitation into intimacy and this call of submission brings me closer to God. And the closer I get to God, the more I long to be completely with God. I am reminded of Paul's writing to the Corinthian Church in *2 Corinthians* chapter 5, where he makes a strong argument for his Heavenly calling. He actually makes the statement that to depart from these earthly bodies is to be swallowed up by life. What a queer statement that is! You mean, that once we depart here, instead of dying, we are actually swallowed up by life? That's exactly what I mean. In that, there is no sting of death. And with that in mind, I can submit myself fully to God, willing to endure any sort of earthly trial which will work out for my good, with the full knowledge that any experience here is only temporary. And Heaven, which is eternal, is my true goal.

This mentality prepares me for any and all trials that may come my way. And just as gold is refined and purified by fire, so also are our lives refined by trials and circumstances. This morning, I was looking over a tree in my yard that is growing quicker and stronger than any other tree around. Do you know why it grows so well? It is because it grows above the sewer line. It is the existence of poop that fertilizes it and makes it grow quick and strong. Our lives are no different. Trials make us stronger. Trials empower us to greater good. And they serve as a testimony of a loving God that stands true to His promises at all times.

Perhaps the hardest thing for me to accept about this new life that Paul talks about in *2 Corinthians 5*, is for me to allow my mindset to be changed into something eternally minded. I war with my flesh every day. I want stuff. And I don't think that there's any amount of stuff that I could ever possess that would satisfy my earthly craving. I want a bigger house, a new car, more technology, etc. ad nauseam. How many things have I asked

God for? Now compare that with how many times I have asked Him to make me just like Him.

Last night, I went to sleep singing, *"Father, make me just like You....Daddy, make me just like You.....I want to be just like You."* I don't know why that verse from Jason Upton came to mind, but it did. And this morning, it gives me hope. It lets me know that my soul will not see corruption. For somewhere, underneath the muck and cravings for more "stuff", lies my true identity. A heart that is willing to be changed and made like the One that laid down His own life for me. And that comforts me and brings peace to a mind that wrestles with distraction.

Today's Prayer
Father, my heart's prayer is to be made just like You. You stand above and beyond all else in my life. I so easily get distracted and entangled with the snares of this world. I lust for stuff constantly. Forgive me for that Abba and remove that log from my eye. I walk around with so many spiritual handicaps. Lord, I need You. I need more of You. I need to be intimately held and known by You. I ask You to heal my wounded heart that has voiced so many complaints before You. Bind me up and by the power of Your Holy Spirit, make me whole. Father, continue to work in my life so that I am less distracted by the things that so many others value. Thank You for what You've

blessed me with. I know that I live a prosperous life. But Lord, help me to not consider those things members of my own body. Help me to not be identified through them. Lord, if they cause me harm, give me the courage to cut them off. I seek only to be identified as Your child. I seek mostly to be known by You and to know You more. This is my request before You today. Use me as You see fit. Change me as needed, for Your glory and for Your use. In Jesus' name, and by the power of His demonstration of love, I pray, Amen!

Day Twenty-Three

Daily Dependence

Today's Word
"Give us this day our daily bread." *Matthew 6:11*

Today's Thought
Part of prayer is our requesting our needs to be supplied by our Heavenly Father. We can take this at surface level, but that will only lead to surface level Christianity. Or, we can truly look into what Jesus is speaking and we will grow and mature as strong as oaks. My prayer for you and I is for us to stand firmly rooted in Scripture. Therefore, let's dive in.

Jesus is making more than just a statement here. The word Jesus uses for bread here is nothing more than a mixture of flour and water which the Jews used to make a loaf. The loaf was about as thick as your thumb and was spread out over a plate or platter. It was not meant to be sliced, but broken. This is the same bread that Jesus used in the Last Supper. After the Last Supper, each disciple took the bread, broke it, and remembered Jesus' body being broken for our needs. That's what sustenance is all about- fulfilling needs. Jesus understood this during His fast in the middle of the desert. Satan came and tempted Him to turn stones into bread. Jesus replied by quoting *Deuteronomy 8:3* saying, *"It is written, man does not live by bread alone, but by every word which proceeds out of the mouth of God."* In the midst of a forty day fast, Jesus was sustained by God's Word, not food.

So, while we can surely pray for God to fulfill our daily needs, we must be able to recognize that our greatest need is the presence of the Almighty within our lives. The Jews would likely remember this through the story of manna. In *Exodus 16*, we are told of how God fed the Israelites in the wilderness daily. Surely, the disciples knew this story well. Each day, as they awoke, the Israelites would arise and gather all the bread they needed to sustain their family for that day. Some required more, others less, but they were cautioned to not take in more than they needed. If they tried to hold more than they needed each day, the next morning worms would overtake it, and it would begin to stink. God wants to provide for us daily. By our continual dependence on Him and Him alone, we learn to trust Him. Withholding more than we need causes us to trust our own judgment, not God's wisdom.

This is also addressed by the wise writers of the book of Proverbs. *Proverbs 30:8-9* tells us *"Remove falsehood and lies far from me; Give me neither poverty nor riches--Feed me with the food allotted to me; Lest I be full and deny You, and say, 'Who is the LORD?' Or lest I be poor and steal, and profane the name of my God."* Do you get it? Falsehood and lies are found within our lives when we hold onto more than God has allotted for us. And this amount is different for every individual. But we must make sure that we are not holding on to more than God has determined to bless us with. By doing so, worms will overtake our possessions and they will be poisoned.

Pride causes us to stand apart from God. If we hold onto more than what God allots for us, we will begin to be full of pride. We will look at all our possessions and say, "Look at the wealth I have obtained. I have obtained this by the work of my hands. I should write a book and tell others about my secret to getting rich." Humility paints the opposite picture. Regardless of the amount of things we obtain, we look around and say, "My, how God has blessed me. God please send someone my way that I may bless today, just as You have blessed me. I want to show them the words written within Your Book, for those words sustain me." One mindset desires to make others like ourselves. The other mindset desires to show others the Christ, so that they can be more like Him.

As I write this morning, I am reminded of an earlier teaching in the *Sermon on the Mount.*

Jesus said that if someone asks you for your coat, give him your shirt also. Again, having a proper understanding of the source of our sustenance allows us to freely give, for we are only stewards of that which God has entrusted to us. Fulfilling our needs and the principle of stewardship go hand in hand. They also bring about a sense of communion that we spoke on yesterday. *Psalms 33:18* tells us *"Behold, the eye of the LORD is on those who fear Him, on those who hope in His mercy, to deliver their soul from death, and to keep them alive in famine."* By hoping daily in the Lord's mercy, we are assured that the Lord's eyes are upon us. And if we keep our eyes upon Him, we can live as Jesus lived. We can do the will of the Father. Is there any greater blessing in life?

Let each of us remember that prayer is communion with God. It is sitting at His table and dining in fellowship and intimacy. In the bilateral communication that we discussed yesterday, let us learn to trust God daily. This is my prayer. It requires submission, but the fruit of that submission is more than any blessing that this world can offer.

Today's Prayer
Father, thank You for teaching me to lean on and depend upon You daily. Lord, I truly find sustenance within You. You not only feed me;

You truly provide for all of my needs. Because You bring me in daily, I am truly learning to trust You. I am discovering many things that I do not entrust to You. Forgive me for holding back. Help me to surrender. As You cause me to be mindful of the things that I so often hold back for myself, bring Your Word to my mind, through the power of Your Holy Spirit, so that I may surrender them to Your Will. Lord, to know You more and to make You known is truly the prayer of my heart. Therefore, I give You my everything. For You are everything to me. In Jesus' name, Amen!

Day Twenty-Four

Forgiveness in Prayer

Today's Word

"And forgive us our debts, as we forgive our debtors." *Matthew 6:12*

Today's Thought

What a strong statement to make in prayer! How often do we pray for retribution, when in fact, we should be praying for forgiveness? How many wrongs have been committed against me? And how often have I brought up those wrongs to God, looking for Him to bring justice instead of mercy? Oh, how we are saints that are still sinners! I pray that we not overlook the importance of this statement that reveals the true heart of Christ!

"Father, forgive our debts just like we have forgiven our debtors." Can I even honestly pray that with a sincere heart? Well, according to Jesus, I better be able to. And if I can't, then I better allow the Holy Spirit free reign to uncover the manipulated Word which lies within me! Again, we are reminded that prayer is as much about changing us as it is about altering our circumstances. It is communion with God. And when we commune with the Divine, we will definitely walk away different then when we entered in. Like time with a true friend, prayer causes us to be better, not by the world's standards, but by eternal standards.

Those that wrong me most, or those who stand adamantly opposed to my own standards, I consider enemies. But this is not so with God. God reaches out to those that consistently wrong Him. He reaches out in love. And that love is the same love with which He embraces His own Son, Jesus. What a paradigm this creates in the Christian's heart. Puzzled, we must begin to look at our enemies as friends that have not accepted our love yet. There is no way for our mindset to change by our own efforts. God must do a work within us which places us on equal and level ground with all of mankind. Regardless of religion, moral turpitude, or ideology, I am a sinner like all of mankind. The only difference between a Christian and anyone else is our acceptance of Jesus and our willingness to submit to Him.

Truth be told, Jesus has no enemies. Others may refuse Him, reject His love, but the entirety of His life was laid down for all of mankind. Some may choose to be enemies of Christ, but that is their choice, not His. Jesus only offers forgiveness. Forgiveness to the point that He was willing to pay the price of their sin whether they accept Him or not. Let's make this practical and not merely theological. What if someone committed identity theft against you. They rob you of all of your personal wealth. They pretended to be you. And they left you penniless. How would you feel? What would you seek in return for their evil deeds? Would you not seek justice? Is this not what each of us have done to Jesus? Have we not made ourselves saviors? Do we not look to our own efforts to bring us closer to God? This is nothing but religious fraud. Only Jesus can bring us into relationship with the Father. Nothing else will do. Our best efforts simply can't measure up.

Jesus tells us to forgive. And those that truly realize how much God has forgiven them cannot help but be willing to forgive others. By realizing my own inadequacies and need for a Savior, I should realize how much others need the same. Who am I to judge? When Paul referred to himself as the chief of sinners in *1 Timothy 1:15*, he wasn't using hyperbole. He realized that the greatest enemy of his own salvation was himself. In the war between the flesh and the Spirit, he was chief. We must mature in our relationship with God to the point that we see the same in ourselves. That kind of perspective relieves us of judgment over one another. And that level of understanding will allow us to pray like our Savior, "Father, forgive me as much as I am willing to forgive." Oh, God, make this a reality in my own heart!

Today's Prayer

Father, help me to find forgiveness in my heart! Help me to have a loving heart like You have. Transform me and my brokenness into something beautiful and pure. I have nothing to offer but my own submission. I need You. I want You. Change me and create in me a pure heart! I need You to do a miracle within me so that I am not threatened by others or myself. Help me to view the world around me as You view it. Help me to see others as You see them, broken but with so much potential, just like me. And as I welcome Your forgiveness, empower me to forgive others. I long to see no man as my enemy. And I need Your Spirit to make this a reality. Fill me up and break the hardness of my heart! Make me like You. In Jesus' forgiving name I pray, Amen!

Day Twenty-Five

I AM Delivered

Today's Word
"And do not lead us into temptation, but deliver us from the evil one. For Yours is the kingdom and the power and the glory forever. Amen." *Matthew 6:13*

Today's Thought
Here, in the close of the model prayer, a prayer that Jesus uses as an example for how we ought to pray, we see what some may say is a contradiction. Jesus asks His Father to not lead us into temptation. Yet, *James 1:12-14* tells us something different. Let's look:

Blessed is the man who endures temptation; for when he has been approved, he will receive the crown of life which the Lord has promised to those who love Him. Let no one say when he is tempted, "I am tempted by God"; for God cannot be tempted by evil, nor does He Himself tempt anyone. But each one is tempted when he is drawn away by his own desires and enticed.

So which is it? Why would God ever lead us into temptation if He promises to never tempt us? God actually uses trials to refine us and to prove His own just character to us. Over and over throughout the Bible, we see God putting men and women into circumstances which are for their spiritual benefit, though it may be contrary to their flesh. If we look only with our humanly near-sighted and faithless vision, we would think that God is setting us up for failure. Nothing could be further from the truth. God only prepares success and prosperity for us.

The difference is how we define success and prosperity versus how God defines it. God defines success not through the currency of money or gold, but through the currency of love. And Jesus said that we cannot love any greater then when we lay down our lives for others. Jesus proved this ultimately through the demonstration of the cross. He took our burdens, paid the price of sin, taking on our shame and guilt. And what was Jesus' heart throughout that process? *"Father, if there is any other way for this to be done, please let this cup pass away from me. Nevertheless, not my will, but only Yours be done."* What a picture of love and faith! What a blessed Savior! The world thought that Jesus had been defeated. His own disciples fled in fear and denied Him. Yet, God had led His own Son into the trial of eternity, knowing that Jesus' Righteousness would be made known soon enough. And all that Jesus had claimed over the last three years would be proven as true. And what is the message that rose forth from the empty grave three days later?   "I love you.   I always have and I always will."

I am reminded of Paul's writing to the Corinthian Church in *1 Corinthians 10:13*: *"No temptation has overtaken you except such as is common to man; but God is faithful, who will not allow you to be tempted beyond what you are able, but with the temptation will also make the way of escape, that you may be able to bear it."*

In this blessed promise, we are assured that God will never lead us into a situation that we cannot overcome.   There are trials in life.   Like James speaks of, sometimes we are led away from God by our own lusts, or cravings for things which are forbidden.   But there are other times when, like Jesus in *Matthew 4*, we are lead into trials by the Holy Spirit.   Remember, this was how Jesus started His ministry.   He started out having to endure hardship and being tempted by Satan. This was not done so that Jesus could have faith; for since childhood, He was filled with fullness in faith.   No, I believe it was done so that Satan would have a realization of just who he was dealing with. And it was done as a demonstration for us, so that we can be assured that the same Spirit which delivered Jesus through incredible temptation can deliver us as well.

Oh, how we **_must_** learn the difference between our leading and God's leading! Our leading ensures our own demise. But when God guides, it leads to blessing. When God called Abraham to take his son Isaac to the top of Mt. Moriah and offer him as a sacrifice, God knew full well what beauty would come from the experience. Abraham struggled, but through faith and trust in God, Abraham followed through. And just as Abraham began to drop the blade onto his son, God provided a sacrifice. Go back and read the story in *Genesis 22*. Isaac continually asked his father about the existence of the sacrifice. And Abraham only responded, "*God will provide.*" And provide God did. And Abraham was made the Father of Many Nations for his faith!

Next, we see Jesus pray for deliverance from the evil one. We must always remember that Satan and his minions seek to steal, kill and destroy. He hates it when servants of the Most High become passionate in their walk with their Maker. It threatens his dominion upon the earth. Therefore, he will do everything he can to get us to distrust God and trust in our own intellect. Is this not what Satan did to Adam and Eve in the Garden of Eden? And they chose demise over blessing. They chose their will over God's will. A cruel God would have never warned them ahead of time about the dangers of the fruit of that tree. A loving Father would warn His children of the dangers of taking of that fruit. And warn, He did. Yet, the enemy of our souls convinced God's first creation to mistrust God and seek their own way, just as he had done. They got that which they craved, but it was for their own demise, not their blessing.

I love how Jesus closes this prayer out! It is closed with a remembrance as to just who holds all the power and control. Jesus' understanding is revealed with the declaration that God is in control. God has it all covered. We don't have to work out the details or win the battle. We need only trust and have faith. For if we can just do these two things that are contrary to our flesh, we will obtain all blessing, power and glory!

In closing today, I encourage you to consider well how you pray. First, know to whom you are praying. Pray with purpose. Make your needs known to God. In the process of prayer, allow God to change your heart. Pray for deliverance. Pray for strength in the midst of trials and for the Holy Spirit to empower you through all circumstances. Don't get overwhelmed, but know that God is ultimately in control. And those things that Satan means to destroy you, through faith, God will actually turn out to be a huge blessing! Have faith my friends. And pray up!

Today's Prayer

Father, You truly are the ultimate demonstration of love. I have never known anything like You. Actually, there is none like You. You alone are worthy of my greatest attention and full devotion. Lord, thank You for blessing me in so many wonderful ways. I need You every hour to continue to work in and around me. Though my circumstances may look dire, and my heart is truly desperate, I have faith that You will bring me through all trials and fires of life without even a single hair being singed. You will deliver me. Your will is to deliver me. You are in control, for You have all power and dominion. You defeated Satan and death through the power of the cross and You will deliver me through all things. So Father, I pray that my life becomes an extension of Your hands. Use me according to Your will so that others may taste the love with which You have blessed me. May my own will decrease so that Your will may increase within me. In the name of Your Son, who is my beloved Savior, I pray, Amen!!!

Day Twenty-Six

The Power of Forgiveness

Today's Word

"For if you forgive men their trespasses, your heavenly Father will also forgive you. But if you do not forgive men their trespasses, neither will your Father forgive your trespasses." *Matthew 6:14-15*

Today's Thought

How many of God's children live in a state of unforgiveness because of our hardened hearts? Jesus had just finished praying the model prayer, and in His heart, He knew that His communion with God was beyond that which most men were willing to understand. Therefore, He provides instruction. What a gracious and patient God we serve! He does not leave us bewildered or left to our own imaginations. He provides clear understanding.

Over and over again, Jesus was asked by His supporters and His detractors alike about the power through which He operated. His answer was consistently the same to all people: "*I only do that which I see the Father doing.*" Jesus' entire life was a model of forgiveness. He forgave sins. He forgave iniquities. He healed the broken hearted and set the captives free. And the ultimate example was His prayer of forgiveness while on the cross: *"Father, forgive them for they know not what they do."*

He that was without sin, took on our sin, so that we might live free. In a sermon by Judah Smith, a beautiful contrast is made. He talks of Jesus standing next to Barabbas while the people cry out for Barabbas to be set free instead of Jesus. You can reference *Matthew 27* and *Mark 15* if you want more of a background here. But what we must know is that Barabbas was an evil man. He was a murderer and the leader of a bunch of rebels. He rightly deserved death by Roman law. Jesus did nothing against Roman law. But He had offended the religious folk of His day. Therefore, the people cried out for the release of Barabbas. Barabbas represents all of us. We are all guilty before God's eyes. Yet, God chooses to take on our sin and extend grace unto us. Like Judah Smith says, *"Jesus knew the will of the Father. For Jesus knew that the Father would have to treat Jesus like Barabbas, so that He could treat Barabbas like Jesus."* Therefore, Jesus remained silent; seeking only one thing, the redemption of mankind.

Though Jesus had not yet tasted sin, He knew that one day He would. He would take on all that was vile and separated man from God. And yet, His heart remained full of love. Think about that.

What if you knew that everyone you ever had relationship with here on this earth would desert you in your darkest hour? Most of us wouldn't choose to remain friends with them, much less willingly become their servant! But here is Jesus, the Creator of the universe, choosing to come to earth and serve the same humanity that would do nothing but spit in His face and reject Him. All the while, His heart was constantly interceding on our behalf. All the while, asking God to look over our sins and rejection of Him. The story seems too good to be true. But isn't that just how God works?

God will never ask us to do something that He is unwilling to do Himself. He will never ask us to go through a trial that He Himself has not endured. Jesus was tempted in all points as we are. He was tempted to be unforgiving and unrighteously angry. Yet, He was without sin. He showed us that through the power of the Holy Spirit, we can be different. We don't have to live like the world lives. We can surpass the righteousness of the religious leaders that are only out for their own gain. We can become servants to humanity. And until we get the understanding that the calling of servitude is the highest and most noble calling that God places on mankind, we will never experience the fullness of God.

This is why forgiveness is so important. Often, we struggle to forgive because others have seriously hurt us. And that hurt goes deep into our hearts. The deeper the hurt, the harder it is to get to the root. But if we are willing, the Spirit will make us able. Oh, how great our need is of such a God-filled mindset in our world of divisiveness! We must learn to forgive, just as Christ forgave. And by doing so, it shall be our own lives that are changed! This is more of what the world around us needs. This is God's calling to our hearts! Serve one another. Forgive one another... For in doing so, we are doing the will of the Father!

Today's Prayer
Father, oh, the bitterness that has taken such firm root within my heart. I recognize my need for the Holy Spirit to have free reign within me! I need You to break away the hardness that surrounds my heart. Help me to forgive to the point that I am willing to extend grace and love to those that have hurt me! Help me to forgive to the point that it costs me something greater than mere words! Father, I know that by allowing this work within my own life, I will be forgiven of my many trespasses against You. Oh, how thankful I am to remain by Your side, broken and mangled by my own self-will, but nevertheless with You. You who makes all things new. Lord, restore my life. Protect me from all evil. Provide all that I need. For in You alone, I place my trust. Through the powerful

demonstration of Jesus, I welcome this into my life. And through His glorious name I pray, Amen!

Day Twenty-Seven

Jesus on Fasting

<u>Today's Word</u>
"Moreover, when you fast, do not be like the hypocrites, with a sad countenance. For they disfigure their faces that they may appear to men to be fasting. Assuredly, I say to you, they have their reward. But you, when you fast, anoint your head and wash your face, so that you do not appear to men to be fasting, but to your Father who is in the secret place; and your Father who sees in secret will reward you openly." *Matthew 6:16-18*

<u>Today's Thought</u>
What an important topic the Lord has brought us to today! Unfortunately, it is a lost aspect of so many Christian lives. In the verses above, the first thing that rises to my attention is that Jesus says, "*when you fast*" and not "*if you fast.*" This implies that fasting should be part of the Christian's life. Therefore, He provides instructions as to how it should be done. For us to see why we should fast, we must look back into the Old Testament; in particular *Isaiah 58*, which is the passage of Scripture Jesus is referencing.

God was giving a message to Isaiah that was to be shared among the people. We will reference *verses 2-7.*

"Yet they seek Me daily, and delight to know My ways, as a nation that did righteousness, and did not forsake the ordinance of their God. They ask of Me the ordinances of justice; They take delight in approaching God. 'Why have we fasted,' they say, 'and You have not seen? Why have we afflicted our souls, and You take no notice?' In fact, in the day of your fast you find pleasure, and exploit all your laborers. Indeed you fast for strife and debate, and to strike with the fist of wickedness. You will not fast as you do this day, to make your voice heard on high. Is it a fast that I have chosen, a day for a man to afflict his soul? Is it to bow down his head like a bulrush, And to spread out sackcloth and ashes? Would you call this a fast, and an acceptable day to the LORD? <u>Is this not the fast that I have chosen: To loose the bonds of wickedness, to undo the heavy burdens, to let the oppressed go free, and that you break every yoke? Is it not to share your bread with the hungry, and that you bring to your house the poor who are cast out; when you see the naked, that you cover him, and not hide yourself from your own flesh</u>?"

So what we see is Jesus approaching fasting the same way that God had Isaiah approaching fasting to the Jews of old. So often, people fast and let others know about their fasting for one of two reasons. The first reason is overwhelmingly self-centered. People fast so that others will take notice of them and prescribe a deeper state of holiness upon them. When we make our fast known before men, it is so that others will think that we are deeply spiritual. But that kind of fasting profits nothing. In fact, it will destroy us. That's what Jesus is addressing to the disciples in the verses of Matthew above. That kind of fasting creates a spiritual pride that leaves us apart from God. That's why God brings this up to Isaiah. *"Why have You not heard?"* That's what the people asked of God. It is because that kind of fasting is for the benefit of self and not God.

The second reason for fasting which is equally wrong, still self-centered and we must be certain to stay away from is that of trying to get God on our side regarding any issue. In *Isaiah 58:4*, God says *"You will not fast as you do this day, to make your voice heard on high."* Fasting should never be motivated by attempting to get God's attention. Oh, how I have misunderstood this in the past! I have fasted as a means of sacrifice before God. But that's not the point at all! We should never fast, or do any means of religious duty, in order to have our voice heard by God. The only thing we ever need to do in order to be heard by God is come into His Presence! We should only do religious duties so that we can hear God's voice! That's what's important. I serve because my heart commands it. And by doing so, I am brought into the Presence of the Almighty.

God says that we are to fast in order to know His heart. That kind of fasting commands intimacy. It is not done before others. So many times, when I hear of saints fasting, they seclude themselves in order to keep their sacrifice secret before men. This, too, is wrong. How does God say we are to use the times of fasting? That is answered in *Isaiah 58:7*. While fasting, or not partaking of normal desires, we are to *share our bread with the hungry, take in the poor and downtrodden, and serve others.* There's no way that we can accomplish this in the proper way unless our hearts are set on God, especially when we're denying ourselves, and that's all that God is after....our hearts.

Fasting is about trust. If we continue on in *Isaiah 58*, we will see that God will provide all that we need when we fast. And the effects of fasting are real. *It looses the bonds of wickedness, undoes heavy burdens of sin, sets captives free, and breaks every yoke.* Those are the results of proper fasting. You see, because we are in the right place spiritually with the Father, God changes us. Because we make our hearts more pliable, God is able to work. God has always chosen to work through men and women in order to create change on the earth. In order for God to work through us, we must surrender ourselves to Him. And surrendering is about the offering of our hearts, not the work of our hands.

The last thing I feel led to share today about fasting is the truth contained in *Mark 9.* In this passage of Scripture, Jesus is questioned by the followers of John the Baptist as to why Jesus and His disciples were not fasting during prescribed Jewish times as they and the Pharisees were. Jesus' answer is clear. He basically replies that they will fast in the future, but as long as He is here with them, there was no need to fast. Why is this? It is because Jesus had already fasted enough for His time on earth. The disciples were first hand witnesses to all the effects of fasting that we spoke of earlier. And sure enough, if we look at the early church in the Book of Acts, we see that fasting was a regular part of their lives. This lets me know that it should be as important to me as it was the early Church. Not to get God's attention, but to bring me closer to God and to make me more like Him.

Today's Prayer
Father, thank You for instructing me through Your glorious Word today! Oh, how my heart loves to understand Your precepts and Your righteous ways! You are so good to me! Help this truth,

which You have made known through the Holy Spirit, to settle deep within my heart. Lord, in the future, as I fast, help me to be a greater servant to others. Help me to honor and reflect Your heart to mankind. So often, I have done "spiritual things" in order to get Your attention. Forgive me for that kind of selfish motivation. Forgive me for my ignorance! Father, You are gracious and kind in Your correction. You do not condemn me for being so foolish. I truly realize that all You are after is my heart. And so, with everything that is within me, I offer You just that. In the words of the old hymn, "Here's my heart Lord, take and seal it, seal it for Thy courts above." Holy Spirit, thank You for revelation. Strengthen me for the Father's service. All of this I pray in the name of Jesus and by the new covenant of His blood, Amen!

Day Twenty-Eight

Jesus and Treasure

Today's Word

"Do not lay up for yourselves treasures on earth, where moth and rust destroy and where thieves break in and steal; but lay up for yourselves treasures in heaven, where neither moth nor rust destroys and where thieves do not break in and steal. For where your treasure is, there your heart will be also." *Matthew 6:19-21*

Today's Thought

It's not by chance that Jesus brings up treasure just after speaking on the subject of fasting. Jesus shares the importance of spiritual growth and then warns of earthly abundance. Oh, what a twisted and manipulated world in which we live! For there are preachers, teachers and evangelists that have made the entirety of their ministries based on earthly prosperity! Woe to such dead teachings! I think of Paul's words to Timothy in *1 Timothy 6:9-10*:

"But those who desire to be rich fall into temptation and a snare, and into many foolish and harmful lusts which drown men in destruction and perdition. For the love of money is a root of all kinds of evil, for which some have strayed from

the faith in their greediness, and pierced themselves through with many sorrows."

There is a stark difference between God making one rich through blessing and one that desires to be rich. The man that God makes rich has the trust of God that he may give it all up in a moment's notice. For the man that God blesses with prosperity understands from where his riches comes. He understands the importance of stewardship. There is nothing wrong or sinful in being wealthy. However, most men and women can not handle the trappings that come with such distraction.

The man that desires to be rich will do whatever it takes to obtain riches. He will leave the God of his Salvation if he thinks that riches will be his reward. What a travesty to have such a temporary mindset! If God ever desires for me to be rich, I pray that my heart would never change. I pray that I would invest in others. I pray that I would give more than I could ever expect to receive back. Is this not the example that Jesus gave us? Did He not offer Himself with nothing expected in return? Is this not the heart of the Father and the Holy Spirit? Our God gives liberally. So also, should we.

By doing this, or adopting this mindset, we are guaranteed by the words of Jesus to obtain eternal rewards that we shall receive in Heaven. I love that Jesus even brings this teaching down to our earthly mindset. Jesus tells us that at most, we will keep the treasure we've earned here on earth for only a few years. But that which we store up for eternity shall never die! What a blessing! What a teaching! Oh, but how near-sighted we tend to be! So much so, that an entire movement has sprung up within the Church that espouses such blasphemy! God doesn't need you to fund His Kingdom! For His Kingdom is found within your own heart! It is funded through the love of God. Remember, God's currency has nothing to do with earthly wealth. God's currency is love.

"And these three things remain, faith, hope and love. And the greatest of these is love." 1 Corinthians 13:13

"For God so loved the world that He gave His only begotten Son, that whosever believes in Him shall not perish, but inherit eternal life." John 3:16

Can we not see the truth of these verses? I tell you this by the Spirit of the Almighty God, have nothing to do with false teachers that encourage you to sow your savings into their ministries. For the real man of God will allow God to put it on your heart to give as He impresses! You cannot buy God's favor! You cannot earn God's love or sacrifice your way into His blessing!

All that we gain here on earth only adds up to rust or dust. What lasts is the relationships in Christ that we build. What lasts is the sacrifice of our time and earthly treasures. I do not want you to hear me wrong in this. When I speak of giving of our possessions, I am not speaking on tithing. For it is our responsibility to support our local church and others that enlighten us spiritually. However, our requirement before God is to give 10% as a tithe to the church to which we belong. Anything beyond that is between you and God, just like fasting. In fact, God encourages us to test Him in our willingness to tithe. Look to *Malachi 3:10* for this truth.

Oh, how convinced I am day after day that God consistently pursues my heart! He wants to do His work within me so that He may do His work through me. This has been my prayer for years: "Lord, do whatever You need to do to me, so that You can do whatever You choose to do through me." This is not an easy prayer to pray. For daily, I am reminded of my own brokenness. I am reminded of my own pride, lust and greed. And daily, I find myself at the feet of the God who gave His all for me, asking for forgiveness and empowerment to live differently. I truly pray that You might enter into this journey as well. For what I have experienced is the most beautiful pain that I have ever known. And that which God is doing within my own heart, which no one else will ever see, is the greatest gift that anyone could ever receive. Oh, brothers and sisters in Christ, hold firm to the truth of the Word and sound teachings! May we all fix ourselves on Jesus alone!

Today's Prayer

Lord, You have truly blessed me in ways that lie beyond my own comprehension. But of this truth I am sure, all that I have tasted from You is good. It brings a sweet satisfaction to my soul. You provide a peace that all of the world's riches could never match! Lord, forgive me for asking for material items so much. So often, I get distracted by the lusts of this world. Forgive me Father! Help me to remain fixed upon Your love which was so richly demonstrated through the life of Your Son Jesus. Keep me in a position of yielding to the Holy Spirit. May every move I make be a reflection of Your goodness, kindness, compassion and mercy! Empower me with grace that I might make You known by my words and actions alike! In Jesus' wonderful and righteous name I pray, Amen!

Day Twenty-Nine

The Battle of Two Masters

Today's Word

"The lamp of the body is the eye. If therefore your eye is good, your whole body will be full of light. But if your eye is bad, your whole body will be full of darkness. If therefore the light that is in you is darkness, how great is that darkness! No one can serve two masters; for either he will hate the one and love the other, or else he will be loyal to the one and despise the other. You cannot serve God and mammon." *Matthew 6:22-24*

Today's Thought

They say that the eyes are windows to the soul. I have seen this saying attributed to everyone from William Shakespeare to Leonardo Da Vinci. It is most commonly attributed to an old English proverb. But I think Jesus may be the originator of this saying. As far back as the Old Testament, we see the importance of our sight and our spiritual understanding. For everyone sees, though everyone may not have their eyesight. Spiritual understanding is the willingness to peer into our own hearts and request understanding from our Creator. And thankfully, Jesus gives us instruction on this issue.

Jesus said the lamp of the body is the eye. Chuck Smith has said that our eyes are like window panes. Whatever prejudices or personal perspectives we have on life create filters through which we see the world. Everything is tinted by how we view ourselves, others and the world around us. So how do you view things? Do you mistrust the world because of past hurts and current fears? Do you doubt what men tell you because you have been let down by empty promises in the past? We must be aware of what we're willing to see... *and what we're unwilling to see.*

When Jesus says that if our eyes are good, our entire body will be full of light, He is addressing the state of our hearts. You see, if I live for love, then my heart will be full of love. I will see others through a filter of love. And I will reach out to others more readily in love. But the converse is also true. If I am only able to see through the filter of hate, pride, guilt, anger, bitterness, jealousy or a multitude of other negative emotions, then I shall see the world around me as against me. I will be more ready to defend my own position than I will to reach out to others. Oh, what a dangerous and manipulated state so many live in!

Recent studies have shown that each person's eyes are uniquely different. Like our DNA, they are unique to each individual. Likewise, our souls are each unique. We are each purposefully created different by God Himself. He cares for each one of us so much that He makes us unique and special to Him. And it is through this identity with the Father, that we shall each find our true purpose in this world. Unfortunately, most people wander through this world trying to be something they're not, or they invest so much time foolishly imitating someone else. How we settle for so much less than what God has for us!

Although we are unique and different from one another, we all share similar characteristics. Without God, our hearts are bent on pleasing ourselves first. But with God, we can obtain a different perspective. You see, we all serve another master. The important question is "*Who do you choose to serve?*" For as Jesus said, no one can serve two masters. Do you serve the god of self, or God Almighty? Whatever master we choose to serve determines our destiny. And by serving God, we will walk where no man can lead us. We will walk with God Himself.

Jesus knew the trappings of success in this world. He warned consistently about identifying ourselves by our worldly position. We must learn to identify ourselves as God sees us. This allows us to be full of light and abounding in love. For when we comprehend that we are loved perfectly by God, all fear will be cast away from us. We will be free to serve others without being afraid of putting too much on the line. We will offer ourselves to others, just as Jesus did, without consideration of the return on our investment. This is the life of the Gospel. Love God and love our fellow man- these are the two great commandments.

Today's Prayer

Father, oh, what a tinted and dingy perspective I so often have on the world around me. As I see so many people living in hurt, poverty, fear and anger, I struggle to find compassion. I hold back because I don't want to expose myself too much, somehow fearing that their misfortune will rub off on me. Father, You are my Protector. I have no reason to fear any person or circumstance. Filter my eyes with love. Help me to see others as You see them. Help me to consistently identify myself through Your perspective. Forgive me for being judgmental of others. Help me by filling me completely with Your precious love. For in Your arms, I have no fear. Therefore, my prayer is that I will not abandon the God of my Salvation. My heart cries out to know and be known fully by You. In Jesus' name, Amen!

Day Thirty

Are You a Worrier?

Today's Word

"Therefore I say to you, do not worry about your life, what you will eat or what you will drink; nor about your body, what you will put on. Is not life more than food and the body more than clothing? Look at the birds of the air, for they neither sow nor reap nor gather into barns; yet your heavenly Father feeds them. Are you not of more value than they? Which of you by worrying can add one cubit to his stature? So why do you worry about clothing? Consider the lilies of the field, how they grow: they neither toil nor spin; and yet I say to you that even Solomon in all his glory was not arrayed like one of these." *Matthew 6:25-29*

Today's Thought

We cannot start today's thought process without rightfully remembering the truth that we learned yesterday. No man can serve two masters. We must consider the beautiful treasure that God is; far more than we concern ourselves with the fading and temporal treasures of this world. With that in mind, this understanding that God cares for us and so our care should be for Him, Jesus instructs us to not worry about our lives. What does Jesus mean here?

He clarifies the thought by bringing up the material possessions that all people need- food and clothing. In Maslov's Hierarchy of Needs, three things are essential to human living- food, clothing and shelter. Jesus is addressing two of these. These things are essential to human flourishing. How are we to not worry about things that are essential? The burning question leads us to the truth of **TRUST**. We must trust *Jehovah Jireh- Our God who Provides*. Like the Jews wandering through the desert on the way to the Promised Land, we must trust that God will fill our every need as we march unto Heaven.

I love how Jesus brings it to the most simple of examples. Look to the birds. Does God not feed them daily? How many starving birds do we see each and every day? I have a friend that has really grasped this understanding. Almost daily, despite any and every financial struggle, I hear of his encouragement to others to simply trust God. What a beautiful testimony! If God loves the birds enough to care for them and provide for them, how much more will He take care, provide for, and cover us daily?

Look to the lilies. Are they not glorious in their color and beauty? And yet, they seemingly rise from nothing. Within only a few short days they grow and blossom before our eyes, reminding us that God prepares the way for our own growth and beauty. If God clothes that which will only last but a season, how much more will He clothe us? Is He not infinitely more invested in our well-being? Oh, that this glory of this truth might settle deeply within our hearts!

Are we not His adopted sons and daughters? Is He not our Abba, our Daddy? You see, we worry because we do not have a close relationship with God. And Jesus, understanding this, is calling the disciples into a closer relationship with Himself. Are these not the very same men that had just days or weeks before left their livelihoods and families in order to follow Jesus at His Command? Is He asking more from them? Yes, He is. He wants them to know that He is not asking them to sacrifice more, but to offer more. He wanted their hearts. Just like He wants ours. And if we are willing to step into the deep waters of intimacy with God, our trust will be secure. For one cannot truly know God without trusting Him with everything that he has. The closer I get, the more I see and understand His love for me. There is no end to this truth. For on this side of Heaven, I will never stop growing.

Therefore, I see worry as an enemy to my soul's growth. And the way I keep from worrying is to press myself deeper into the bosom of God. One of the greatest expressions of intimacy in this world is the act of making love between a husband and a wife. Chest to chest, in the warm embrace of one another's arms, there is complete trust and transparency. Oh, though this truth warms our hearts, we must know that this is only a shadow of the type of relationship to which God calls us. Our hearts must be set on becoming so close to God that though we are two separate beings, in intimacy, we become one. And as we continue in this understanding, we are willing to be more transparent with one another. I learn to trust Him by offering my heart to Him. It is my faith that feeds this passion I have for Him. For He has never let me down. He has never forsaken me; even though, I almost daily forsake Him. What a beautiful God, who is the lover of my soul!

Today's Prayer
Father, thank You for sharing this beautiful truth with my heart today. Lord, You speak into the intimate parts of my heart that cause me to be overwhelmed by Your Love. There is truly none like You. Nothing compares to the love You have for me. Abba, I give myself to You. I love You so much and yet I understand that there is so much about You that I still have to learn. God, I trust You. I trust You to provide for all my needs. I will do my best to care for all that You have entrusted unto me. Help me to be a better steward. I want my life to be a light that reflects Your glory. I need You minute by minute, and I know that this is not

too much to ask, for You desire to know me this well. God, You are truly beautiful. Bless me as You see fit, for You only have my best interests in mind. In Your blessings, I am content. Simply to be Your servant and the servant of others around me, this I pray for strength and willingness to do. In Jesus' name, who is my truest example, I pray, Amen!

Day Thirty-One

Don't Worry....Be Happy, Happy, Happy

Today's Word
"Now if God so clothes the grass of the field, which today is, and tomorrow is thrown into the oven, will He not much more clothe you, O you of little faith? Therefore do not worry, saying, 'What shall we eat?' or 'What shall we drink?' or 'What shall we wear?' For after all these things the Gentiles seek. For your heavenly Father knows that you need all these things. But seek first the kingdom of God and His righteousness, and all these things shall be added to you. Therefore do not worry about tomorrow, for tomorrow will worry about its own things. Sufficient for the day is its own trouble." *Matthew 6:30-34*

Today's Thought
Building precept upon precept and line upon line is the way that God takes us deeper into relationship with Him.　Yesterday, I made the following statement: *Therefore, I see worry as an enemy to my soul's growth.　And the way I keep from worrying is to press myself deeper into the bosom of God.*　This understanding is paramount to today's teaching.　Worry is an enemy to our souls.

Jesus confirms this by letting us know that God will take care of us. *1 Peter 5:6-7* tells us this: *"Therefore humble yourselves under the mighty hand of God, that He may exalt you in due time, casting all your care upon Him, for He cares for you."* We humble ourselves by running into the arms of our Father. Most people seem to think that humbling yourselves is about diminishing your own importance. That couldn't be further from the truth! Humbling ourselves is about realizing just how important God is. Do you see the difference? If we choose to address humbleness by looking at our own inadequacies, the focus is still on us. And that's the definition for pride, not humility.

We must remember that this teaching of Jesus is one of the first, if not the first, serious teachings that He chose to share with the disciples. He is letting them know about the journey to come. For the next three years, they would walk with Jesus through some incredible highs and some desperate lows. Their lives would be flipped upside down as Jesus continually taught them to walk by faith and not by sight. There is so much more to this journey with God than many are willing to endure. But for those that endure, theirs is the blessing of the abundant life.

Our lives with Jesus are no different. Faith in Christ does not promise us that we will never endure hardship, pain or suffering. But it does promise us that we will never walk alone. God will bring us into a closer relationship with Him. He will place people in our lives that will endure tough times with us. This is the testimony of all people of faith. Faith strengthens us and gives us what we need to continually press on. Worrying does the opposite. It keeps us focused on our problems instead of the God who provides solutions to every problem. That's why Jesus points us back to the Kingdom of God.

"Seek first the Kingdom of God and His righteousness..." Oh, how important this statement is! Remember, the Kingdom of God that Jesus is referencing here is not Heaven, it lies within us. When we enter into relationship with Jesus, He plants the seed of the Kingdom of God within our hearts. It is up to us to build ourselves up through the reading of the Word, to be washed by the power of the Holy Spirit, and to walk in His Righteousness. The prophet Isaiah says, *"We are all infected and impure with sin. When we display our righteous deeds, they are nothing but filthy rags. Like autumn leaves, we wither and fall, and our sins sweep us away like the wind."* (*Isaiah 64:6 NLT*) Why then should we ever seek our own deeds and accomplishments to justify ourselves? No, seek God and His Righteousness.

We close today's devotional with another important truth: Don't be so concerned with tomorrow that it makes you ineffective today. How many people get paralyzed with fear over things out of our control? Jesus teaches us that there is enough to be concerned about in the present. Showing concern and worrying are two different things. Be mindful of the circumstances of your day. Take opportunities to bless others in the present. Seek God in the present. For none of us has control over tomorrow or the circumstances that may arise. But all of us can have an impact in the here and now. This is why it is wrong for us to continually put things off. Don't wait for tomorrow to reach out to that person who is hurting today. Don't convince yourself that tomorrow you'll get back to pursuing your divinely implanted passions. Take advantage of the moment that is before you. Seek the Lord while He may be found.

Today's Prayer
Father, thank You for the gift of today. Thank You for reminding me that You have all of my needs in mind. Because You are focusing on my needs, I can focus on others' needs. Empower me today to fulfill the Great Commission by reaching out to those that are lost and hurting around me. Give me wisdom in how to love others so that they would know just how much You love them! Oh, how I long to be salt and light in a world that

needs You! I cannot do this by any of my own efforts, so I place all my trust in You. Speak to me and through me. Help me to be Your hands and feet in a world that is full of destruction, divorce and separation from You! I offer You my life today. May Your Kingdom be made evident in my heart today! Holy Spirit, I yield to Your wisdom, power and guidance. In Jesus' name I pray, Amen!

Day Thirty-Two

Who am I to Judge?

Today's Word
"Judge not, that you be not judged. For with what judgment you judge, you will be judged; and with the measure you use, it will be measured back to you. And why do you look at the speck in your brother's eye, but do not consider the plank in your own eye? Or how can you say to your brother, 'Let me remove the speck from your eye'; and look, a plank is in your own eye? Hypocrite! First remove the plank from your own eye, and then you will see clearly to remove the speck from your brother's eye." *Matthew 7:1-5*

Today's Thought
If there were any one thing that the modern Church needs to really work on concerning the world around us, I would say that this principle needs some serious consideration. Christians of our current culture, mostly due to our voting stance regarding morality, are called the Religious Right. And within our society, there is a seeming great divide between the religious folk and the secular. The secular people often state that the religious folks' most easily recognized quality is their judgement. And with institutions out there like Westboro Baptist, and other churches which haven't received publicity for their views, who can

blame them? We may not throw out such vehement hatred as Westboro Baptist, but how often do we judge others? How do we find balance between judging others for the sins they commit and not condemning them to Hell for doing them?

We must recognize that the journey of faith is one of a personal nature. When Jesus addresses the Kingdom of God, He lets us know His desire is to set up His Kingdom within our hearts. When Jesus addresses sin, He wants us to consider our own sins first. If we judge, we will be judged. So we should not judge others. However, proclaiming truth is not judgement, it is simply sharing truth. But we must always be carefully to never proclaim a truth that we have not first accepted for ourselves. Let's look at an example.

Jesus instructs us to not proclaim to others about the piece of sawdust in their eye when we have a six foot long 2 x 4 piece of lumber protruding out of our own eye. That's a pretty graphic description. And I don't think He's using hyperbole here. Realize that He just stated that with whatever measure we choose to judge others, we ourselves will be judged likewise. For if we know the truth, and yet continue to sin, how much more evident will our sins be before God and mankind? But the neighbor, which may not have tasted of God's sweet love, his sins are small in nature; because to him, they may hinder his enjoyment in life, but they are not a handicap! However, I would challenge any of us to walk around with a six foot piece of lumber protruding from our eyes and live any sort of normal life. And yet, so often, spiritually, we do just that. Who am I to judge?

How easy is it to recognize the sins of others and not address my own sins? It's human nature. Think back to the Garden of Eden. When Adam was confronted about eating of the forbidden fruit, did he take responsibility for his actions? No, he blamed Eve. He said, "*It was the woman that You gave me that told me to eat.*" He tried to take the spotlight off of himself and shift it to someone else. Oh, how often we do this and don't even realize it! If Adam's heart would have been right, he would not even felt the need to blame Eve. He would've simply admitted his wrongdoing. Is this not what salvation is all about? Jesus took our sin and shame on the cross while praying for our forgiveness. He knew our sins, and His heart was not to condemn, but for our eyes to be opened to the truth of His love.

Remember back to when you first said yes to Jesus. Perhaps you were standing in the midst of a large group of people. For me, I was at church camp and only twelve years old. There I stood with the conviction of God pouring down on me.

My heart was beating fast, for I thought at any second all of my sin was about to be made known before everyone! I was so convicted about my own sin that I did not even consider the sins of everyone else around me. I just knew that in that moment, I needed forgiveness. I needed a Savior! And so, despite my fear of judgement of all others around me, I went forward and told the preacher that I needed Jesus in my heart. You see, my own sin was evident to me above and beyond the sins of anyone else. How do we move away from such wonderful perspective? *"Oh, now, I am saved.....therefore I should try to save the rest of the world!"* Oh wretched man that I am, who will deliver me from the bondage of this death? Can I not see that it is myself that still needs my utmost attention? Does my own heart not turn away daily from the God that I love? Do I not look upon others with judgement in my heart and perhaps even hatred? Oh, God, how I long to be free from this sinful nature of mankind!

Notice how Jesus turns the events in the passage of Scripture above. In verse 5 above, Jesus says, *"Hypocrite! First remove the plank from your own eye, and then you will see clearly to remove the speck from your brother's eye."* Who's removing the speck from our brother's eye? We are! For we are to not judge, but assist. One can only stand in judgement when he stands apart from the one he is judging. Does a court judge not sit at a distance and above all others in the courtroom? Jesus basically tells us to not sit in a place of authority over others casting judgement on them from afar. Instead, consider and address your own sin, remove the handicap from your own life, then you can go and assist your brother with that which he needs.

An easy way to for you and I to determine if we are judging others or not is by looking at our willingness to work alongside and assist our neighbors and loved ones in need. Jesus proved that He did not come to the world to judge us. He did this by living amongst us for more than thirty years while doing nothing but proclaiming God's love and reaching out to those in need! And so often, we're unwilling to offer ourselves to others for one hour of needed help! Oh, the spiritual planks that we walk around with! May God forgive us for not being more like Jesus! The Spirit is willing, but the flesh is weak! I don't know about you, but I think I need to go look in the mirror and address some things!

Today's Prayer
Father, forgive me for being so judgmental of others. So often, I am more concerned with proving that I am right than I am seeing all my wrongs. I need Your help. This old sinful nature dies hard! I so often think thoughts about others that aren't blessings, they're curses. Forgive me

and wash me clean of such things! Lord, with Your Word in my heart and the Holy Spirit alive and well within me, I know that I can do this. I know that You will empower me to live different from the rest of the world. And You can cause me to still be approachable and loving, not casting judgment or condemning those around me. Father, may I never lose remembrance of the innocence I had when You first called me into relationship with You. I knew nothing. I accepted You like a child. Father, keep me in that place of relationship with You. Protect me from making things so complicated. I simply need to know You more each and every day. Help me in this. Help me to be more compassionate and giving to my fellow man. In Jesus' name, and by the power of His example, I pray these things in confidence, Amen!

Day Thirty-Three

Be Wise, But Not in Your Own Eyes

Today's Word
"Do not give what is holy to the dogs; nor cast your pearls before swine, lest they trample them under their feet, and turn and tear you in pieces."
Matthew 7:6

Today's Thought
Proverbs 3:7 instructs us to not be wise in our own eyes, but respect God and depart from evil. We respect God best when we heed His instruction, when we yield to the Holy Spirit, and when we accept friendship with Jesus. That's what this Sermon on the Mount is all about. Jesus is instructing the disciples on the proper way to live. He is changing all that they've ever trusted in. And He's doing it sentence by sentence. Jesus was just talking about judging others, and then He throws in this sentence which seems to call us to judge others. Is this not contradictory?

It's not. Let me explain why. In *Matthew 7:5*, Jesus had just said that we need to address our own issues rather than focusing all of our attention on others' issues. And then come the verse above. *"Do not give what is holy to the dogs; nor cast your pearls before swine."* Jesus is warning us that there are things that the Father will share with us that is for our own benefit. These blessings are pearls of wisdom, and they are indeed holy. They are unique for each one of us, and their uniqueness declare His love for each if us individually. But if they are so beautiful and filled with such wisdom, why should we not share them with others? It is because others may not be in the place to hear them. Those with whom you choose to share God's truth may not be in a place of understanding.

My wife and I were talking the other day about a disagreement I had with someone. She watched as another person spoke some things that were untrue. I listened intently to what the person was saying. And then, I carefully invited the person with whom I was disagreeing to see things from a different perspective. They refused. They were adamant that they were right. Therefore, I told them that I would consider what all they had said more deeply and I offered no more. I knew that anything else would have only divided this person from me. What good would that do? Is it more important that everyone around me always understand that I think I am equally right? I tell you the truth when I say that the Holy Spirit was working through me. I am sure that I had experienced this same situation years before. And the old me would have stood there and argued until it ended in bitter disagreement. I have watched as relationships with friends and loved ones disintegrated due to my own pride. I have witnessed myself being so determined to share the truth of God with others when they weren't in a place to hear it that it caused division between us.

So, we are not to judge others, but we are to use proper judgment. In other words, we are to constantly yield to the Holy Spirit. Doing this will keep us from going too far with the Word. Look at the life of Jesus. He never sent anyone away. He answered questions that others asked Him in very simple terms. Others went away from Jesus sad because they weren't willing to do all that He asked, but it wasn't He who pushed them away. Their own hearts directed them away. He always invites us in. And if we are willing to come into relationship with Him, He invites us to go deeper. He asks us closer. Is this not a model for our own relationships?

Notice that Jesus also warns us in the verse of *Matthew 7:6*. If we share things with others that are not in a place to hear them, those people that we are trying to help will turn on us with anger and bitterness. And they will seek our demise. They will do all they can to turn and tear us to pieces. Relationships will be severed. So even if we have removed the plank from our own eyes, and we notice the speck in our brother's eye, we must be very careful about how we assist them in removing it. Oh, what a message this is for all modern day teachers of the Word! It is also a word for all of us that love our brothers and sisters enough to invest ourselves in other's lives. Wisdom comes from God. Therefore, we must continually submit our hearts to Him. And by doing so, we will not only gain wisdom, but also the wisdom of how to best love those that God has placed in our lives. Now, that's Kingdom living!

Today's Prayer

Father, thank You for loving me well. You provide wisdom and understanding. You help me relate to others in such a way that they may experience You. You love me and those in my life so much. As I read and contemplate Your Word, I am convinced more and more of Your intense love and desire for full relationship with us! You amaze and overwhelm me. Yet, at the same time, You remain so constantly intimate with me. You remain real and tangible to me. Father, I am so in love with You. I yield myself to You today. Help me be a picture of love and acceptance to those I work with and am in relationship with today. Help me radiate Your love and an invitation into relationship with You today. Empower me by Your goodness. In Jesus' name, Amen!

Day Thirty-Four

Ask, Seek, Knock; But for What?

Today's Word

"Ask, and it will be given to you; seek, and you will find; knock, and it will be opened to you. For everyone who asks receives, and he who seeks finds, and to him who knocks it will be opened." *Matthew 7:7-8*

Today's Thought

Oh, how manipulated this verse has become in the modern excessive culture of America! We use this verse to justify our desire for more things. And that is the last thing that Jesus is talking about here. Jesus is continuing to instruct the disciples on Kingdom living. And that type of lifestyle has very little to do with what we own, but what mostly about what we cherish. So what do you and I cherish? What is it that our hearts long for so strongly that we seek God and His Word to find the promises which can guarantee them for our present and our future? This question cannot be properly answered without first considering our past.

We give very little thought as to how much our past dictates the desires of our hearts today. If we have been brought through the trials of abuse, we seek trust. If we have struggled through years of financial debt, we seek financial freedom. If we are able to realize the tremendous sin that we have been rescued from, then we will begin to desire holiness. And that's what Jesus is instructing the disciples on...holiness. He just finished telling the disciples to not be frivolous or incautious with the things of God which are holy. Why then would we think that He would be reverting back to any type of materialistic mindset? The simple answer is, He's not!

James 4:3 tells us that we ask and don't receive because we ask amiss. There is a very big difference between asking for the things of God which will bless us and asking God for things which will curse us. Many times, through much of my own financial despair, I have asked God why I shouldn't win the lottery, or why I haven't already come into tremendous financial wealth. If I've asked and haven't received, it must be because I am asking for something out of His will. For if it is God's will for me to be wealthy at this point in my life, there is nothing that could keep God from pouring out His financial blessings upon me! God will take care of my needs, and I trust Him implicitly for them. But I know, without a doubt, that God wants the entirety of my heart. And until you and I can, without compromise, hand over everything that is most precious to us, we will remain to fall short of the Kingdom living into which Christ invites us.

Jesus promises us that if we ask, seek and knock, we shall receive, find and doors shall be opened. So instead of questioning God as to why we have not received, our time and efforts are best spent investigating our hearts and motives. We must begin to live as Jesus lived. We must do those things which we see the Father doing around us. We must love as He loves. We must have compassion as He has compassion. We must serve as He serves. Then, and only then, will we begin to ask and seek for the right things. Subsequently, the doors shall be opened up.

So instead of asking for the things which only amount to rust and dust, let us learn from the example of Solomon and begin to ask for wisdom. For we know that God will give wisdom liberally to all those that ask (*James 1:5*). Is this not the Apostle Paul's heart toward the Church? *Colossians 1:9-12* tells us this about Paul's heart: *For this reason we also, since the day we heard it, do not cease to pray for you, and to ask that you may be filled with the knowledge of His will in all wisdom and spiritual understanding; that you may walk worthy of the Lord, fully pleasing Him, being fruitful in every good work and increasing in the knowledge of God; strengthened with all might, according to His glorious power, for all patience and longsuffering with joy; giving thanks to the Father who has qualified us to be partakers of the inheritance of the saints in the light.*

This should be the continual prayer of all saints. Not only for ourselves, but for one another. In a world filled with war, death, sickness, despair and loneliness, God can use more servants of this mindset. That, my friends, is what God is calling you and I to. He doesn't need us to be rich, He needs us to be full of understanding of His will for our lives. He doesn't need us to be promoted, He needs us to simply serve. And if we are willing to enter into this same mindset that other saints of faith in years gone by have, the world will surely not be the same....and neither will we.

Today's Prayer

Father, I need wisdom in my life. I need desperately to know Your will each and every day. On my own, I am destructive to myself and those around me. But with You, I am an overcomer. In You, I have peace. Lord, do a work within my heart and fill me with wisdom. Come Holy Spirit, and quicken my inner spirit to be full of light and willing to operate in Your glorious gifts. I submit myself to You. And I ask You to use me according to Your will alone. Empower me by Your Grace. Strengthen me as only You can. In Jesus' wonderful name, Amen!

Day Thirty-Five

How Much More?

Today's Word
"Or what man is there among you who, if his son asks for bread, will give him a stone? Or if he asks for a fish, will he give him a serpent? If you then, being evil, know how to give good gifts to your children, how much more will your Father who is in heaven give good things to those who ask Him! Therefore, whatever you want men to do to you, do also to them, for this is the Law and the Prophets." *Matthew 7:9-12*

Today's Thought
What powerful statements from the Master! And yet, I feel that we lose the importance of such strong words. Building on past understanding, we must realign our mindset to thinking about the "more" Jesus is talking about. As a father myself, I think often of the things that I want to provide for my children.   I spend much of my time and resources doing what I can for them. But there is no gift I can give them that is greater than faith, hope and love.   That's what I pray over my children. That's what I long for each of them to experience to the fullest extent.

And if I, a man who battles constantly between the things of this world and the higher calling in

Christ Jesus, long to give such wonderful gifts to my own children; then imagine how much God longs to do for us! How then, can I remain so temporarily minded when it comes to my own trust in God? Why do I grow so disheartened when there seems to be more month than the money will provide for? Why do I always keep my eyes on my own failings as opposed to the generous provision of my Master and Savior, Jesus Christ? It is because, like everyone else in this world we live in, I don't submit myself to God in the right way.

There is an aspect of devotion and service which is wonderful and lasting. And there is a part of me that likes to relish in the immediacy of my own obedience. I like to know what God wants me to do, so that I can go and do it. I like to put a checkmark in that box so that I can look up to my Father and say, *"Hey, I did that, just like You told me to. Aren't I a good boy?"* What a devastating and destructive mindset to have towards God! But it's there. Right beneath the surface, and I fight it continually. Why?

Does my life have to be based on a performance based model continually? No. In fact, if I remain in that mindset, then everyone else in my life will be judged by me based on my own performance standards. This has been one of my biggest struggles in my life. My own expectations of my wife and children, extended family and friends alike, to meet up to the standards that I think are appropriate.   And when they don't meet the standards that I am imposing on them, I grow frustrated, disheartened or angry. That leads me to feeling unloved and wronged in some way. And it all is a lie! It couldn't be further from the truth!

As I look to the words of Jesus this morning, I am reminded that I simply cannot make it without Him.   Regardless of how much I meet up to my own expected standards, or the standards laid before me in the Word of God, I must remain focused on the good gifts. Faith, hope and love. This is what I choose to align myself to each and every day. *Am I being faithful to my calling of being a child of the Almighty? Do I remain in hope to experience a touch from my Father each and every day? Do I give and receive love, just as I ought to, without preconditions or measurements of performance?* Let's explore.

Am I faithful to my calling of being a child of the Almighty?   Faith.   We can't know God without it.   It is the means by which God communicates with us and forms our relationship with Him.   Just as a child is birthed from his mother, so also are we each born again as a new creation when we release our lives to Jesus. A child cannot dictate his birth. He doesn't ask to be created. He is simply created. And he is dependent on the provision of his parents. This is how we are to relate to our Father in Heaven. Not as a bratty teenager, but as a dependent infant. Oh, how quickly so many saints lose this mindset and move into the demanding and independent teenage years in our relationship with God! As I grow older, I truly realize my own need for dependency on God. For years, I have asked Him why He had not delivered on all of His Promises. All the while, He was. He was giving me the good gifts instead of the curses I was demanding.

Do I remain in hope to experience a touch from my Father each and every day? There is a stark difference between the days that I speak with God and the days that I don't. There is a different mindset, and a different way of living that I experience. Experience has taught me that when I lean into the Father as soon as I awake, my day goes smoother. I think less about me and more about others. Life may throw some crazy curveballs my way, but somehow, I'm equipped for the chaos. I'm ready and willing. I love to see God move in miraculous ways. But so often, Christians desire to see supernatural circumstance; and we don't even realize the supernatural experience that we have available to us each and every day! Through the power of the Holy Spirit and the demonstrated love of Christ, we can enter into God's Presence boldly, without reservation. With no prior notice, no scheduled appointment, we can speak to the Father of all Creation and crawl into His lap, tell Him that we love Him, and expectantly look forward to His genuine love in return! It doesn't get any more miraculous than that!

Do I give and receive love, just as I ought to, without preconditions or measurements of performance? As I touched on earlier, so much of my life has been performance based. I have to remove this mindset from me daily. Better said, I have to ask God to help me remove it, for on my own, my efforts are futile. In my natural state, I love others because they first love me. I do good to others to repay them because they have already blessed me. And if I forget to repay someone else's good deed? Oh, the frustration and self-condemnation I put myself through! But that's not how love truly works. That's what we've grown accustomed to in a world that doesn't know God intimately, but that doesn't make it right. We are to love as God loves. Give and be free to receive. No preconditions means that I will not try to judge someone else's motives as to why they are bestowing love upon me. I will not second guess their heart's motives. I will simply accept it and relish it! And no performance measurements means that I will not say just what constitutes love and what doesn't. I will simply accept it. And I will relish it!

Jesus ends the verses we are looking into today with a reminder to His disciples. *"Whatever you want men to do to you, do also to them."* For this is what all of the Law and testimonies of the Prophets have been saying all of these years. If you want mercy, show mercy. If you want love, show love. For whatever standard we set upon others, including God, that is the same standard that we each will be judged by. Oh, how this makes me realize my need for daily dependence on God! I am so ill-equipped for Kingdom living without Jesus in my heart daily! This is the point of Jesus' words. If we are willing, then He is surely able. All we have to do is submit. Ask Him to change us, and He will do it. We can live a more noble life. We can live a more abundant life. But the only way to get there is through submission and servitude. With this in mind, have a very blessed day indeed!

Today's Prayer
Father, oh how much I depend upon You! For by my own means, I am wretched. Without You and Your Divine guidance, I am as lost as a ball in high weeds. I need You today God. Daddy, would You revive this soul once again and make it shiny and new? Would You help me to rid myself of my own performance based standards of love

and living?   Help me God, for I cannot do it without You. I have spent so many wasted years wrestling with so many things that You can remove in an instant.   Yet, like a dog to its own vomit, I have so often returned to my own mess. Father, forgive me and wash me clean. Make me more like You. I offer You my life. I submit my will to You. Help me to not be judgmental, but to love as You love. Give me all the good gifts that You have had prepared for me since the foundations of the world were laid! Oh, how I long for Your goodness in each and every moment of my day! Therefore, I submit and welcome Your blessings. In Jesus most wonderful name, Amen!

Day Thirty-Six

Should We Be Surprised?

Today's Word
"Enter by the narrow gate; for wide is the gate and broad is the way that leads to destruction, and there are many who go in by it. Because narrow is the gate and difficult is the way which leads to life, and there are few who find it."
Matthew 7:13-14

Today's Thought
The financial guru Dave Ramsey has a saying, *"Live like nobody else today so that you can live like nobody else tomorrow."* I like that saying. It encourages people to not fall into society's trap of keeping up with the Jones'. He encourages people to get debt-free as soon as possible, and then learn to live by paying cash for everything. Most people cannot even imagine what that kind of living is like. And for many, like me, past decisions have wrought my ability to do just that. Strangled by student loans, a mortgage, and just keeping things going around here makes me feel as though I'll never get over the hump. It feels like a continuous uphill battle. Often, I become frustrated and look to God for rescue. He always provides, but the way has remained difficult. Instead of further frustration, should I really be surprised?

The Christian life is not much unlike the saying that Dave Ramsey uses. Our tomorrow is eternity. And my continuous hope is in my eternity where I will never taste want, need, despair, pain, frustration, broken-heartedness or any other thing that seeks to steal my joy. Therefore, I continually invest in that tomorrow as opposed to spending the majority of my time and resources on the fading things of this world today. Jesus spelled it out clearly. Yet, many Christians wrestle daily with maintaining the proper mindset. This must change. And as always, change is best when it begins in ourselves.

Jesus was a black and white kind of guy. He spelled things out which left very little room, if any, for the grey areas where so many seem content to live. For years, I lived my Christian life still entrenched deeply within the ways of the world. Im not saying I'm perfect now, for my sins are great. But there is a vast difference between the sinner that chooses to remain in sin and the sinner that is willing to submit to the authority of Christ daily.

I had a sleepless night last night. And when I awoke this afternoon, several bills still need attention, my back was still screaming in pain, and my heart was heavy with life. But I sat down and declared, "*I am a chosen child and servant of the Most High. Father, I submit myself to You this day. Use me according to Your will. Empower me with Your Grace and accompany me throughout this day.*" I didn't plan that little prayer. It just came to my heart. And that little prayer of a willing heart is what God is looking for. My circumstances haven't changed (*YET!*), but my heart and mind are united with my soul which brings me peace and comfort. That's a different way of living. That's *Kingdom* living.

So, as Christians, should we really be surprised when things are difficult and our paths are tough? Jesus clearly tells us in the verses above that the His gate is narrow, few people will find it, and the path beyond that gate is difficult. But that is the path which leads to life. The easy road that most people find is broad, and its' walk is much easier. However, that road leads to eternal death. Jesus reinstated this truth when He spoke to His disciples about the last days of this world. In *Luke 17:33*, He says, "*Whoever seeks to save his life will lose it, and whoever loses his life will preserve it.*"

The path of Christianity is one of servitude. The Christian is commanded to think about others before self. And that means that Christ must put us in the path of others. Most of us like to pick and choose to whom we will share God's message of grace and love. But we must be sold out to God to the extent that we are willing to go as He directs. That means that we might endure some great personal tragedy and tremendous hardship by the world's standards. But God looks at our present circumstances with a compassionate hope. His compassion never fails, so He always remains in that spot of pain with us. But He remains hopeful because He knows that the personal pains are developing us into the crafted tools of His hand. He knows that these things which the Devil means for our demise and harm will make us more useful for the Kingdom.

This testimony which He is building within us, which tells of His unfailing love and continual provision, might be the very thing that pierces another's heart and brings them into relationship with Him. Can one put a price on a man's soul? Then why would we be so surprised when part of that price is some temporary discomfort which will work out for God's glory? Our job is to trust and obey. Therefore, I remain submitted daily.

Today's Prayer

Father, I echo the prayer which You brought to my heart this morning. You know my personal needs and my desires. I want to taste of Your goodness today. I want to see Your provision. Lord, heal my heart that is so easily distracted and ensnared by the entanglements of this world. Keep me from the broad road which leads to destruction and death. I choose to walk this narrow path with You because it not only leads to something greater than anything this world has to offer, it fuels me each and every day. Your Presence is my passion. And because You are willing to meet with me this day, I thank You. I submit my life and will to You. Use me according to Your purpose and accomplish within and through all that You truly desire. In Jesus' name and by the power of His glorious demonstration, Amen!

Day Thirty-Seven

A Cautionary Word to the Believers

Today's Word
"Beware of false prophets, who come to you in sheep's clothing, but inwardly they are ravenous wolves. You will know them by their fruits. Do men gather grapes from thornbushes or figs from thistles? Even so, every good tree bears good fruit, but a bad tree bears bad fruit. A good tree cannot bear bad fruit, nor *can* a bad tree bear good fruit. Every tree that does not bear good fruit is cut down and thrown into the fire. Therefore by their fruits you will know them."
Matthew 7:15-20

Today's Thought
Jesus continues on these foundational truths to His new disciples with the five verses above. He just warned us about the difficulties that we will face in this world. On that note, yesterday, after openly airing my own dirty laundry about struggling financially, I watched a video of a Coptic Christian Church in Egypt being burned as hundreds of Islamists shouted "Allah Akbar." The Holy Spirit quickened my soul to my own selfishness while my Christian brothers and sisters are literally fighting for their lives and for protection of their houses of worship. Oh, how narrow-minded and selfish our American mindset

can be! God forgive me! I ask you to join with me and many others that are praying daily for persecuted Christians around the world.

On to today's focus... Jesus warns us of false prophets who will have the appearance of ourselves, yet they seek personal projection and disregard the harm they do to the Body of Christ. Oh, how much we see this in today's church! We see and hear of the scandals within the Church's walls....televangelists that make a mockery of the Gospel and prey on the poor people within the world's landscape. There's some good Christian ministry on television and radio today; but oh, how we must be careful as to who we give our eyes and ears to! Thankfully, Jesus helps us to identify who is real and who is not. By their fruits you shall know them.

If you need to know the difference between a minister of God and a false prophet, all we have to do is look to their lifestyle and their lives. I'm not suggesting that a minister should not live a good and financially secure life, but if I'm living above the majority of my congregation's means, then there's a problem. Preparing for this devotional today, my heart has been broken while doing research over the amount of people that have left the Church, or have been swindled out of millions of dollars because of the so-called "prosperity doctrine". Entire churches have collapsed under the weight of such lies. Let me ask you this: If Jesus wants everybody to be rich, then why would he warn us that it is easier for a camel to enter through the eye of a needle then it is for a rich person to enter into heaven? Not everyone can handle riches. Likewise, not every Christian can handle wealth. Jesus doesn't condemn the wealthy, but He definitely offers some strong warning against seeking wealth and the trappings of riches. The important question for each of us is: *"What is my heart's longing?"*

To the best of my recollection, the men in the Bible that God blessed with tremendous wealth, never sought it. They simply sought God. I do not read of David asking God for financial increase in the Psalms. I do not remember Abraham asking God for more "stuff." Solomon asked for wisdom and because his heart was right, God empowered him with more wealth than even his father David had. And even with man's greatest wisdom, Solomon still lost sight of God in his pursuit of more. Oh, friends, we must get this right. God cares not about our pocketbooks and wallets, but He is always concerned with our hearts.

The Apostle Paul offered Timothy clear instruction in *2 Timothy 3:12-13*: *"Yes, and all who desire to live godly in Christ Jesus will suffer persecution. But evil men and impostors will grow worse and worse, deceiving and being deceived.*" The "false prophets" that Jesus is referring to are deceiving others because they are deceived themselves. They have an appearance of godliness, but their hearts are not founded on the foundational truths of Christianity. They claim that their success is due to God, but it is more due to natural talents, good communication skills, and charisma. Oh, how my heart breaks for the false prophets within the Church! For as the Bible says, "*The teacher will receive the stricter judgment.*"

The encouragement for you and I today is that Jesus will prepare our hearts for those that He chooses to instruct us through. And we must ensure that our hearts are lined up to His Word so that we can tell the difference between the righteous and unrighteous. If my heart is set on becoming wealthy, I am easy prey to a false prophet proclaiming seed-sowing faith. And if I think that for a second that I can buy a divine miracle, then I'm not aligned with God's Word. We must be thankful for what we have and be prepared for all persecution. We must remain vigilant so that we are not caught off-guard or unaware. And that is done best by daily time with our Father, a heart that is inclined to His Word, and a willing Spirit within us. That is my prayer for myself and anyone who reads these words. May God encourage each of us in our pursuit of Him.

Today's Prayer

Father, thank You for convicting and instructing my heart today. Lord, I am thankful for all that You have provided me with. My heart knows You to be gracious and merciful. You always provide. My heart is heavy this morning as I think about the persecuted Church around the world. Lord, forgive my selfish ways of thinking of myself first. Be with those that need You for their survival. Help them maintain the faith in a real way that continues to convert the lost and those that even persecute them, for You took Saul who was the Church's greatest persecutor and molded Him into the Apostle Paul. Do that in our day Lord. Break the hearts of those that seek the Church's demise. Father, thank You for wisdom concerning false prophets within the Church. Guard my eyes and ears and keep me from ways that lead toward self-promotion and self-glorification. For You alone are worthy of my greatest praise. You alone are my Salvation, my Light, and worthy of all my praise. In Jesus' name, Amen!

Day Thirty-Eight

Work Out Your Own Salvation

Today's Word
"Not everyone who says to Me, 'Lord, Lord,' shall enter the kingdom of heaven, but he who does the will of My Father in heaven. Many will say to Me in that day, 'Lord, Lord, have we not prophesied in Your name, cast out demons in Your name, and done many wonders in Your name?' And then I will declare to them, 'I never knew you; depart from Me, you who practice lawlessness!'" *Matthew 7:21-23*

Today's Thought
I cannot read these words of Jesus without thinking of the letter that Paul and Timothy wrote to the Church in Philippi. In *Philippians 2:12-16*, Paul encourages the Church in the following manner: "*Therefore, my beloved, as you have always obeyed, not as in my presence only, but now much more in my absence, <u>work out your own salvation with fear and trembling</u>; for it is God who works in you both to will and to do for His good pleasure. Do all things without complaining and disputing, that you may become blameless and harmless, children of God without fault in the midst of a crooked and perverse generation, among whom you shine as lights in the world, holding fast the word of life, so that I may rejoice*

in the day of Christ that I have not run in vain or labored in vain."

You see, there are a couple of things which continually stand out to me in the verses of Jesus above. First, it is not enough to say that you are a Christian, for any person can do that. It is those that live out their lives in relationship with God that will taste eternity with Him. Being a Christian means that we have Christ within us. This is not a commitment of the head, but one of the heart. Second, it amazes me that God loves you and I so much that He is willing to work through those that do not have relationship with Him in order to show His mercy to others. I'll explain this further in a moment, but this is why Paul and Timothy encouraged us through their words in the book of *Philippians* to work out our own salvation with fear and trembling, for it is a very serious thing.

Before we go about questioning our own salvation, let's not read more into Jesus' words here than He is presenting. We know that our relationship with God is based on faith. And that can be a difficult journey for the most devout of Christians. Jesus tells us that all we have to do is ask Him into our hearts and He will enter in. We simply need to truly acknowledge our need for a Savior, our own desperate failings in comparison to God's holiness, and then repent from our evil ways and live as Christ taught us to. That's part of the reason why these words from Jesus' Sermon on the Mount are so important to our spiritual foundation. They are paramount. We must let these words pass through the difficult and treacherous eighteen inch path from our heads to our hearts. For when we taste their goodness, life truly changes within us. We will begin to welcome servitude to Christ instead of resenting it. We, like Paul often did, will begin to refer to ourselves as bondservants, or servants that choose to remain under the command of our Master. Oh, what a wonderful calling it is to be granted such a blessing!

Notice that Jesus says, "*Not everyone who says to me Lord, Lord, shall enter into the Kingdom of Heaven.*" It's not about what we are willing to speak or do, but what we are willing to experience personally. There are those that have and will work many miracles in the name of Christ, those that have and will prophesy and encourage the Body of Christ, and those that have and will cast out demons in the name of Jesus; yet their own hearts remain far from Jesus. Oh, how tragic it must be to witness the strength of God's power only to never experience it personally. If God can speak through the mouth of an ass, like is recorded in *Numbers 22*, then He can certainly speak through the mess of a man like me. But that doesn't mean that I am guaranteed salvation. If my heart is not set upon God as my Master,

Savior, Redeemer and friend; then I am still lost, regardless of how much good He chooses to work through me. Therefore, I must always keep my heart set on God. For that continual relationship encourages my heart that I am in His will.

Each and every day, I am reminded of my consistent need of God in my life. Every day, I am convicted by the power of the Holy Spirit concerning how easily I can slip from living in the will of God to fulfilling the lusts of my own flesh. Now does that mean that I must be saved daily? Certainly not! For the Word is clear that Jesus died once and for all people! But each day, I must be reminded to submit my heart to God so that I can remain in His calling. By doing so, I welcome His load and His burden. And His load and burden is usually either about helping me confront my own issues that keep me from growing closer to Him, or they are in some form or fashion about loving others more. I must love people like Jesus loves them. And I can only do that if I have first accepted His love within my own heart. That's the good taste that I spoke about earlier. May we ever remain focused on such wondrous love!

Today's Prayer
Father, You amaze me with how concerned You are about my own heart. Why then should I pay

such little attention to it? Oh, how often and easily I am distracted away from the things that concern You. Forgive me for my own inconsistency. And in the same breath, I thank You for always remaining consistent and near so that I am never without You or Your instruction. Thank You for offering Yourself to me. You do not seek to destroy, but bless. You do not seek to steal, but to give. You do not seek to kill, but give life. What a wondrous God You truly are! Lord, may the truth that You have delivered unto me today by the power of the Holy Spirit and Your Holy Sword, which is Your Word, permeate deep within my soul. Help me to remain ever vigilant. I ask You to invade my walls of privacy and help me to tear down the things that keep me from being fully relinquished unto You alone! I find it my greatest joy to be Your child. In this, I am content. Bless me according to Your will, and use me as You see fit. In Jesus' name, Amen!

Day Thirty-Nine

The Firm Foundation

Today's Word

"Therefore whoever hears these sayings of Mine, and does them, I will liken him to a wise man who built his house on the rock: and the rain descended, the floods came, and the winds blew and beat on that house; and it did not fall, for it was founded on the rock.   But everyone who hears these sayings of Mine, and does not do them, will be like a foolish man who built his house on the sand: and the rain descended, the floods came, and the winds blew and beat on that house; and it fell. And great was its fall." *Matthew 7:24-27*

Today's Thought

I absolutely love the picture that Jesus paints in the verses above. He uses a clear example to explain the importance of these teachings which we have been covering over the last month or so. We know Jesus to be our firm foundation. And if our lives are built upon His teachings and relationship with God through Him alone, then we shall remain firm regardless of what rises against us.   There are some important lessons to be gleamed here, so let's dive in...

Jesus says that whoever hears His words and does them, that person shall remain firm. If we look fully into the life of Jesus, we will see that there were many people that heard His words, but very few actually did as He said. Even one of those closest to Him betrayed Him due to his desire for a few pieces of silver. Jesus is giving as solemn a warning as He possibly can about the importance for you and I to digest His words and begin to operate just as He operated. Jesus does not ask us to do something that He Himself was unwilling to do. Jesus set the example for us, and then left us the Holy Spirit so that we could be empowered by the Father, just as He was, to live differently.

Jesus also says that whoever hears His words and does not do them, that person will be overtaken and destroyed by the circumstances of life. And then Jesus uses language that can only be described as exclamatory: "*And great was its fall.*" Jesus is telling us that there's more at stake here than just survival in this world. There are eternal ramifications to our decisions made in the here and now. The wise man will hear, do, and live; while the foolish will hear, ignore and perish. Oh, how many people miss this important statement of Jesus! They remain near to the teachings of Christ, yet they never actually enter into relationship with Him. We can surround ourselves with Christians and church all of our lives, but if we never submit to the teachings of the Master and accept His salvation, we will still remain lost. Proximity has nothing to do with salvation. It is about a willingness to submit to He that is greater than I.

There is another point that we as Christians often miss in this teaching of Jesus. Notice that the wise man and the foolish man both encountered the same storms of life. They are both beaten by the elements of life. The difference is in who remains firm and who is destroyed. So many Christians have been wrongly instructed that because we surrender our lives to Jesus, we shall never encounter hardship, tragedy or difficulty. Oh, how contrary this type of teaching is to the words of the Master! We must prepare ourselves for hardship. Paul reiterated this understanding in his second letter to his spiritual son Timothy. *2 Timothy 2:1-3* states: *"You therefore, my son, be strong in the grace that is in Christ Jesus. And the things that you have heard from me among many witnesses, commit these to faithful men who will be able to teach others also. You therefore must endure hardship as a good soldier of Jesus Christ."*

Part of being a Christian is our willingness to stand firm in Christ when we encounter the difficult things of this life. When we experience death of those close to us, we must remain firmly in the embrace of our Savior. When we go through trial and tribulation, we must trust continually in the words of our Savior who tells us that we will not be overtaken. Becoming an accepted child of God is about salvation from our state of sin and becoming children of light. It is not about removing us from an ever-darkening world. As Christians, we are promised hardship. However, that hardship will never be beyond what the Holy Spirit empowers us to bear. And we shall never be destroyed.

When people ask me why bad things happen to good people, I reply that it is because bad things happen to bad people. In every difficulty, there is a lesson to be learned. And every hardship is a calling of the Master into deeper relationship with Him. We started this teaching on the Sermon on the Mount being constantly reminded that accepting the Kingdom of God into our hearts means that our world will be turned upside down. So much of God's way is contrary to that which we desire. But if we remain close to Him, our circumstances may not change, but our desires will. We will learn to accept difficulty, all the while embracing the Father. Is this not what Jesus demonstrated in the Garden of Gethsemane when He prayed, "*Nevertheless, not my will but Yours.*" Let this mindset, which empowered every thought of Jesus, become fixed in our hearts and minds as well.

Today's Prayer

Father, thank You for the promise that no hardship will ever overtake me or destroy me as long as the eyes of my heart remain fixed on You. Lord, You empower me to be an overcomer. You shine brightly upon me so that regardless of the hardship that I may encounter, I shall shine brightly as Your reflection. This reflection of Your love will bring others into relationship with You. Oh, what a glorious and loving God You truly are! God, forgive me of the messes that I have made on my own, for I am sure that they are more than I can even number. Wash me of my iniquity so that I can reflect Your love without spot or blemish. Lord, I humbly and fearfully accept Your calling on my life to be a servant to others. Help me to embrace all that You have purposed in my life. And through that embrace, I know that I will experience more of You. Father, You are enough. Keep me from the distractions of this world which permit me to settle for so much less than You have to offer. May this word, that Your Son Jesus stated for my benefit, permeate the depths of my soul so that they are recalled to my memory in the midst of every hardship and struggle! I will remain firm because my foundation is built on nothing less than Jesus and His Righteousness! I will lean on Your everlasting arms because within Your embrace, I am made whole. Thank You for loving me and molding me as You do. In Jesus' name, Amen!

Day Forty

Let There Be Light

Today's Word
And so it was, when Jesus had ended these
sayings, that the people were astonished at His
teaching, for He taught them as one having
authority, and not as the scribes. When He had
come down from the mountain, great multitudes
followed Him. *Matthew 7:28-8:1*

Today's Thought
Genesis 1:3 says "*Then God said, "Let there be
light"; and there was light.*" There is not a greater
verse to sum up the teachings that Jesus has
shared in what has become known as the
Sermon on the Mount. *John 8:12* tells us: "*Then
Jesus spoke to them again, saying, 'I am the light
of the world. He who follows Me shall not walk in
darkness, but have the light of life.'*" In the
beginning, Jesus spoke light into existence. And
His words here penetrate our hearts so that we
can be brought to life. Light exposes. It brings
understanding and perspective. And as we close
out this study of the Sermon on the Mount, we will
have missed the entire point if our hearts are not
enlightened by what Jesus has shared.

When Jesus finished this teaching, the people
were astonished. I included *Matthew 8:1* in the

verses above because it provides further understanding as to what has just happened. As Jesus came down from the mountain, multitudes followed Him. But if we look back to where we started, we will see that Jesus didn't start our speaking to the multitudes, He started by speaking to the disciples. *Matthew 5:1* says "*And seeing the multitudes, He went up on a mountain, and when He was seated His disciples came to Him.*" Jesus, after seeing the multitudes, was moved with compassion and realized that He must give His disciples a deeper level of understanding. And so He began teaching.

What began as an intimate teaching, we now realize has drawn the multitudes to the mountain top with Jesus and His friends. What a powerful realization! Jesus had no problem drawing a crowd. Whether it be His words, the miracles performed through His hands, His rebuke of the religious folk, or His embrace of little children, everything about Jesus draws us in closer to Him. Why is this? Because Jesus lived transparently. His heart was set on revealing the heart of His Father. And His Father's will is for us to simply live within His firm embrace. People are drawn to Jesus because we experience love when we are close to Him. Oh, how much ministers of the Gospel can learn from this timeless truth! We don't need to have a better marketing plan to get people in the pews. We can't blame a distracted world. If we aren't drawing a crowd, we're not sharing the love of the Father. Why? Because all people long to truly be loved.

I love that Matthew understood what was so different about Jesus. People were astonished by Jesus because He taught with authority. The same being that spoke light into existence more than four thousand years earlier, now is speaking enlightenment into the hearts of men. Matthew recognized the situation for what it was. It was the glorious revelation of truth from a sincere servant who spoke with authority. Jesus didn't teach like the the scribes and Pharisees. They spoke about the outward man. They taught on the importance of looking holy. But Jesus teaches us how to be holy. And that is by letting His words plow through our heads until it reaches our hearts. Where others manipulate, Jesus motivates.

When God put it on my heart to study through these several chapters of Matthew, I was impressed by how many saints in years gone by had been so heavily impacted by this initial teaching of Jesus. Men like A.W. Tozier, Dwight L. Moody, Dietrich Bonhoeffer, and Andrew Murray have all written about the importance of these foundational truths. And at the conclusion of this study, I know why they spoke of it's importance. I could literally spend the rest of my life only taking in these words, and would never exhaust their full meaning. The more that I look into these words, the more I am brought to the realization that I need them to take deep root in my heart daily. The words within *Matthew 5-7* teach us the basis of our faith.

Many times during this study, you have heard me speak of how different life can be if we are willing to live like Jesus. Is that not the definition of being a disciple? A disciple becomes like the teacher. This is the purpose and goal of our relationship with Jesus. He wants to transform all that we are into all that He knows we can be. He gives us beauty in place of our ashes. He brings light to our darkness and peace to our weary souls. And all we have to do is submit. He offers salvation unto all that are within an earshot of His voice. But it is up to you and I whether we will hand over all that we are. I encourage you today, just as I encourage myself, that we would hand over the entirety of our lives to the One that gave up the entirety of His life for us. May God bless the reading and understanding of His Word.

Today's Prayer
Father, take these words of Your Son Jesus and let them continue to astonish me. Lord, may these words take deep root within the fertile soil of my heart. And the hardened places within me, I ask for You to gently turn over the soil and break

my hard-heartedness. Father, I need You so desperately. I am lost without You. You are my light and my salvation, whom shall I fear? Heal my brokenness and align my heart to Your uncompromised truth. I am not willing to settle for less. For I have tasted and I've seen the beauty of knowing You intimately. Enlighten me Father....give me Your eyes and speak to and through me for the entirety of my days. Lord, I submit myself to You today. Use me according to Your will and purpose. In Jesus' most wonderful and fully authoritative name I pray, Amen!